❧ IRISH COTTAGES ❧

❧ IRISH COTTAGES ❧

Photographs by WALTER PFEIFFER

Text by MAURA SHAFFREY

Foreword by ALICE TAYLOR

TED SMART

For Patrick — M.S.

For my children — W.P.

First published in Great Britain in 1990
by George Weidenfeld & Nicolson Limited
Orion House, 5 Upper St Martin's Lane, London WC2H 9EA

This edition produced for The Book People Ltd,
Guardian House, Borough Road, Goldalming, Surrey GU7 2AE

British Library Cataloguing in Publication Data
Shaffrey, Maura
    Irish Cottages. — (Country Series)
    1. Ireland cottages
    I. Title II. Series
    941.50824

Half-title page: Near Lough Gill, Co. Sligo

Title page: Derrylicka, Co. Kerry

Contents

Author's Acknowledgments

I would like to thank the following individuals and organisations for willing help and information: the owners of the cottages I visited; Ellen Cooper; Colin Grant for helpful co-operation; June Eiffe; Dorothy McWhirter; Michael O'lAlmhain; Nicholas Robinson; Gráinne; the Commissioners of Irish Lights; the Office of Public Works, in particular John Cahill; C.I.E. Archivist, Michael Foley; Muckross House Research Library for information on Deenagh Lodge; the District Council of Strabane, N.I.; the Ulster Architectural Heritage Society; the Department of the Environment, Northern Ireland, for information on Sion Mills and Dromore. I would also like to thank Patrick and Cliodhna for patiently reading the draft text and Kathleen Murphy for typing it.

ATLANTIC OCEAN

Map of Ireland to show the location of places illustrated in this book.

IRISH SEA

ATLANTIC OCEAN

Malin Head
Rockstown Harbour
Lenan Head
Horn Head
Muntermellan
Bloody Foreland
Meenaclady
Errigal
Slieve Snaght
Lettermacaward
Glenties
Lough Swilly
Ballyliffin
Urris Hills
INISHOWEN
Lough Foyle
Dunfanaghy
Magheraroarty
Glenveagh Estate
Letterkenny
Lough Finn
LIFFORD
Strabane
DERRY CITY

DONEGAL
DERRY
ANTRIM

TYRONE
ANTRIM
BELFAST CITY
OMAGH
Lough Neagh
Drumbeg
Crossgar
Ballynahinch
DOWNPATRICK

FERMANAGH
Lough Erne Lower
ENNISKILLEN
Lough Erne Upper
ARMAGH
DOWN
ARMAGH
MONAGHAN
Carlingford
Ballymascanlon
DUNDALK
Carlingford Lough

LEITRIM
SLIGO
Lough Gill
SLIGO
Lough Allen
Lough Icey
CAVAN
Lough Gara
CARRICK-ON-SHANNON
MONAGHAN
LOUTH
CAVAN

MAYO
Lough Conn
CASTLEBAR
Clew Bay
Westport
Croagh Patrick
Lough Mask
INISHBOFIN
Claddaghduff
Letterfrack
Streamstown Bay
Clifden
Ballyconneely
Lough Inagh
Maam Cross
LETTERMORE ISLAND
Lettermore
Costelloe
INISHMORE
INISHMAAN
INISHEER
Fanore
BURREN
Doolin
Liscannor
Milltown Malbay
GALWAY
GALWAY
Lough Corrib
Kiltoom
Lough Ree
ROSCOMMON
ROSCOMMON
LONGFORD
LONGFORD
Lough Sheelin
Lough Derravaragh
MEATH
Mullagh
Lough Ramor
NAVAN
Lough Owell
Ballynegall House
MULLINGAR
Lough Ennel
WESTMEATH
TULLAMORE
OFFALY
Lough Dera

CLARE
ENNIS
Sixmilebridge
Bunratty
LIMERICK
Askeaton
Adare
Croom
NENAGH
Newport
TIPPERARY
PORT LAOISE
LAOIS
Abbeyleix
Durrow
Castlecomer
KILKENNY
Dunnamaggan
Clough
Ridge
Muinebeag
Fennagh
Borris
Enfield
Clonsilla
Carton Estate
Ravensdale Estate
NAAS
DUBLIN
DUBLIN
Old Conna Estate
Enniskerry
Poulaphuca Reservoir
Powerscourt Estate
KILDARE
Kildare
Kilcullen
Athy
CARLOW
CARLOW
Old Leighlin
Shillelagh
Carnew
Ashford
WICKLOW
GLEN OF IMAAL
Kiltegan
WICKLOW
Rathdrum
Ferns
Enniscorthy
Ballaghkeen

NEWTOWN SANDES
Newtown Sandes
LIMERICK
Cahir
Ballyporeen
CLONMEL
Belline Estate
Owning
Piltown
WATERFORD
Castleboro Estate
WEXFORD
WEXFORD
Clearistown
Blackwater
Kilmore Quay

TRALEE
WATERFORD
DUNGARVAN

GREAT BLASKET IS.
Dingle Bay
Macgillycuddys Reeks
Kenmare Estate
Killarney
Lough Leane
KERRY
Derrylicka
Sneem
Blackwater Bridge
GARINISH IS.
Kenmare River
Castletown Bearhaven
Bantry Bay
Dunmanus Bay
Mizen Head
Schull
Crookhaven
Union Hall
Rosscarbery
Myross
Castletownshend
CORK
CORK CITY

0 10 20   40   60   80 | km
0   10   20   30   40 50 | miles

Foreword
by Alice Taylor

Sometimes known as a Welsh dresser, this was an important item of furniture in the cottage kitchen. Both functional and ornamental, it was generally made of deal timber, the lower part having doors to a closed cupboard with drawers above. The upper part had open shelves on which to display the 'delph' and sometimes hooks on which to hang cups. The two chairs in this kitchen are also made of deal and are painted. Traditionally, they would have been left unpainted and scrubbed clean from time to time. Both doors are of sheeted timber. The entrance door is sheeted, ledged and braced. The floor is flagged.

Nonie's cottage, like herself, was small and welcoming and exuded warmth. She lived a few fields away from my grandmother's farmhouse. During the summer holidays I often stayed with my grandmother and every Tuesday we took two large baskets of eggs from the free-range hens down to Nonie's cottage, where they were collected by the egg man. As we came into the shadowy quietness of her cottage, Nonie would swing the black heavy kettle on to the iron crane over the blazing fire in preparation for tea. Then, straightening up, she would come down the little kitchen with outstretched arms and enfold me in a comforting hug. To Nonie, my mother was still a young woman, so this made me think that Nonie was very, very old, but she had none of the austerity of my grandmother and always called us children her *leanaí* ('little ones'). Her snow-white hair was coiled in a knot on top of her head, but little white tendrils escaped and framed her face in a soft halo. Because she and her daughter were its only occupants, and both were fine-boned and dainty as delicate china, the cottage had the aura of a feminine haven. Long white nightdresses edged with lace often blew on the clothes line or hung airing by the fire, beside hand-embroidered pillow cases and lace table-cloths. Crocheting and lace-making were Nonie's great love and her high-necked white blouses were always edged with lace; around her shoulders she wore a black crochet shawl and her long black satin skirt swung clear of her tiny black soft leather boots. Her little boots were polished to such a high shine that I could see the firelight reflected on her toe-caps. Her daughter cycled daily to work as a cheesemaker in a creamery ten miles away and back every night, so she was the breadwinner and her wages, together with Nonie's pension, maintained them in a reasonable degree of comfort.

The inside of the cottage, like the outside, was whitewashed, and the yellow thatch came down snugly over the windows like the peak of an old man's cap, sheltering the windows like small deep-set eyes. In the thatch over the door grew a rosette-forming evergreen house-leek which flowered in the summer. As well as looking and smelling good it had an accompanying legend that it prevented bad luck from entering the house and safeguarded against fire. A half-door, while leaving in the fresh air and sunshine, kept out the multi-coloured hens that pecked industriously on the cobbled yard outside. When Nonie wiped the breadcrumbs off the table into her cupped fist, she tossed them over the half-door to the hens outside who squawked in disagreement over the biggest crumbs. The little window in the front only partially lighted the kitchen because the three-foot-thick mud walls funnelled the light, leaving some of the kitchen in shadows that were diffused by the flickering firelight and the light from over the half-door.

On the back wall opposite the window was Nonie's dresser, having the ingenuity of design that provided a decorative showpiece for her entire kitchen collection. The large brown and blue dishes stood at the back of the centre shelf, while smaller plates backed the ones above and below; basins and jugs of various colours stood on the shelves, while smaller jugs and cups hung off the hooks on the shelf fronts or rested in nests of saucers between the basins. The two drawers beneath the wide base separating the top and bottom held all the cutlery, while in the open space below stood the black iron pots and kettles for the open fire. As well as the practical need it fulfilled, Nonie's dresser was a pleasure to look at, with its lustre jugs and flower-patterned bowls. One jug in particular was my favourite. It was cream-coloured with a scatter of pale pink roses and a pink rim and handle, and in this Nonie kept the goat's milk. She had only a small green patch of grass at the front of her cottage, so the goat grazed the long acre together with the donkey which provided Nonie's means of transport. The donkey cart sheltered in the open shed at the end of the cottage, its orange shafts and wheels contrasting vividly against the black rick of turf beside it.

At the lower end of Nonie's kitchen a door opened into a small bedroom, and apart from this all the living was done in the kitchen. The little house was heated by two turf fires for which the turf was cut and drawn from the nearest bog. As the man in the house had died many years before, any work requiring male muscle was done by the neighbouring men. It was part of the interlaced system that prevailed at the time and helped those within it to support each other.

Nonie's cottage was a social centre for those going to and coming from town. Walking down the hilly roads, strong boots and protective clothing were needed, and as Nonie's cottage was on the side of the main road it was used as a changing depot. Often bicycles were parked against the donkey cart rather than pushed up a steep hill on a dark, wet winter's night. She provided numerous cups of hot, sweet tea coloured with goat's milk and crisp brown bastable bread (baked in a pot on the open fire) and if stronger sustenance was required you got a speckled brown egg standing in a blue china egg-cup.

Now the smoke no longer curls from the chimney of Nonie's cottage, for the roof is long gone and the birds build their nests in the ivied gable end that stands as a monument to a noble people who lived in those mud cabins. They were the farm workers who, having no land of their own, helped the farmers till the land. In a primarily agricultural country it was the only means of livelihood available to them. These were the ordinary people of Ireland who, together with the tenant farmers, died of starvation by the roadsides of Ireland during the famine of 1847. Others boarded the coffin ships and sailed for America and Australia, many dying in transit. Of those who made it to a new land, many never returned. Today their descendants come back looking for their family roots amongst the grey stones of Galway and the green hills of Kerry.

Those who survived those terrible times in Ireland became the heart of rural life, their roots buried deep in the soil of the countryside. Some lived on in their thatched mud cabins, while others moved into the cottages built by the British Government at the beginning of this century. Accompanying most cottages was an acre of land which they tilled intensively and which provided all that was needed for the kitchen table. If their needs were greater than their acre could supply, they got the use of an adjoining farmer's field. It worked on the basis of a gentlemen's agreement and served both sides well provided that both sides behaved like gentlemen. The design of those cottages varied very little throughout the countryside. They were small, compact, well-built houses with a high-pitched slate roof and at the front two windows, one on either side of the front door – though sometimes the two windows were together, to the right or left of the door. The door opened straight into the kitchen, which had an open fire at one end, over which a black iron crane stretched. Off this hung the kettle and cooking pots. Around this fire the family gathered at night as this was often the only source of heat in the cottage.

These people, some of whom still lived in the cabins but the majority in the cottages, were a tough and great-hearted people. They had to be tough to eke out an existence on what was available to them, but their great hearts gave them broad vision. Because their ancestors had suffered much and survived, they knew that they too were survivors. Because of their Celtic origins, a love of music and dance flowed through their veins. Fiddle, concertina and melodeon music, some plaintive and haunting, some bubbling with laughter and gaiety, filled the low-ceilinged cabins and cottages, while the people beat out the rhythm of their hearts in the set-dancing on the stone floors of their mountain homes. The cottagers held what they termed 'house dances' where the music, singing and dancing were local and spontaneous and the people gathered in from the surrounding countryside. They nurtured and cultivated the old customs of our race, for the cottages of Ireland were the storehouse of our traditional singing and dancing.

Emigration had always been part of Irish life, and when economic depression peaked, as it did in the 1930s and 1950s, so did emigration. Many of the children from our cottages emigrated to England and America and sent home much-needed money. Young boys from the bosoms of large families and close communities went to the wild and lonely plains of Oregon, where they herded sheep in total isolation for many months. What terrible loneliness must have eaten into the marrow of their bones. And when the dollars came back across the Atlantic to help those at home, was it ever realized what a price in human suffering was paid for them? Girls from quiet hills arrived at Paddington station to work to pay the passages of younger sisters and brothers, either to join them or to go further afield to America. When returning Americans come tracing their long-lost ancestors we might bear in mind that it could be that the dollars of their forefathers kept the heart alive in rural Ireland.

Very few Irish cottages are now in their original state. The economic boom of the 1970s blew out gable ends for extensions and the little cottages mushroomed into much larger homes. Some were abandoned for modern, labour-saving bungalows, and now you will see in rural Ireland the shells of little cottages standing like ghosts in the shadows of new houses. The people who are now seeking out these cottages to restore them are often returning emigrants or people fulfilling a dream of escaping from the stress of living in the fast lane. But the important thing is that our Irish cottages should be alive with the sound of human voices and have smoke curling from the chimneys, not dotting our landscape like quiet grey shadows of another day. Any cottage that sheltered many generations has a past, and there is about an old cottage a sense of timelessness and relaxation that enriches the lives of the occupants. Old stones that have absorbed years of living, sunshine and rain make soothing companions.

Memory on its
Soft grey clouds
Wafting through the rooms,
Webbing here
The part of me
That belongs.
The living that was blended
Through these stones,
So I take with me
Past soul of this house,
And leave behind
Part of mine.

From *Close to Earth* by Alice Taylor (Brandon, 1988)

CLOUGH,
Co. Kilkenny

Take two cottages on a bend in a road, add a pump and a seat, anchor them with a fingerpost sign and you have a meeting place. Here at Clough neighbours must have gathered for decades to fetch water and to chat.

Introduction

S*mallness is the keynote* of a great deal of Ireland's charm. Small-scale buildings, miniature versions of the impressive building achievements of the United Kingdom and mainland Europe, are indeed friendly and captivating. Among the country's surprising number of traditional buildings that still survive to be enjoyed are a great number of cottages. They range from simple one-room houses to extended 'linear' houses, from model cottages built by public authorities to classical-inspired urban terraces.

Today in Ireland there is a growing interest in buildings as an important part of the country's history and heritage. Those who live in traditional cottages may – understandably – find themselves torn between respect for the past (sometimes manifested as a rather romantic nostalgia) and a desire for modern comforts. Deep-rooted folk memories of the harsh conditions in which our ancestors lived have also undoubtedly led to many cottages being abandoned or altered almost beyond recognition. Such vernacular buildings, humble as they are, are not only lovely in themselves but are also a significant part of our social history. They deserve our understanding and our protection.

Whatever their merits or demerits, cottages provided homes for large numbers of people over the centuries, and indeed still do. They sit comfortably among their surroundings in a way that their modern counterpart, the bungalow which has spread so rapidly in Ireland during the past two decades, never will. The one was to do with living, and its appearance was determined by the needs of the occupier, while the other imports a higgledy-piggledy jumble of materials and styles, with cavalier disregard for the spirit of place.

A country cottage was the home of a rural worker: an estate or farm labourer, crafts person or county council employee. Cottages in towns were the homes of artisans or city estate workers. Local authorities, transport companies and mill owners provided cottages for workers and their families who might otherwise have found difficulty in providing their own. In bigger towns the army built terraced homes for soldiers, and after the First World War paired cottages were built for returning soldiers in the outskirts of some towns. The lighthouse and coastguard services built cottages attached to their stations in coastal settlements, and even institutions such as gaols and mental hospitals sometimes built their own cottages. Terraces of cottages, scaled-down versions of formal city terraces and squares, were built to cater for a rising middle class society, particularly in Dublin as the city expanded in the nineteenth century.

The small to medium-sized farmhouses of what would be called 'strong farmers' are also included here, though their owners would never consider them as cottages. These, which include the classical 'box' house, form such an important and ubiquitous part of the traditional landscape that it is impossible not to consider them.

Some cottages were more fanciful. Built for the well-to-do and influenced by the romantic and picturesque principles of the late eighteenth and early nineteenth centuries, these became permanent homes, summer lodges or houses for visitors. On the great estates fishing lodges, shooting lodges, tenant farmers' houses and follies such as shell cottages were all designed as ornaments in the landscape.

This book does not aim to be a comprehensive study of the many and various manifestations of the Irish cottage, but it sets out to convey some of their intriguing variety, their captivating charm, and the great practical possibilities they offer today's home-owners – if only they will take the trouble to recognise them.

The Traditional Irish House

This small three-room house with its unattached outbuilding stands on the windswept Inishowen Peninsula. The chimney stack rises from the kitchen, and the projecting area beside the gable in the foreground is the bed 'outshot'. A typical feature of Donegal houses, this nook, big enough for a double bed, was always positioned by the hearth to take advantage of the heat without encroaching on important social space. It was screened from view by curtains. The entrance porch is at the opposite end of the kitchen and has a separate flat roof, while the main thatched roof extends to cover the 'outshot' projection. The stone walls were painted annually with limewash. The cottage stands on a smallholding and the owners' meagre income would be supplemented by fishing and by the breadwinner's migration to Scotland.

The Irish cottage, as seen throughout the island, evolves from two distinct traditions, the linear and the classical. The former, which derives from ancient origins is the true vernacular style, while the latter, which goes back only to the eighteenth and nineteenth centuries, has its origins in the formal principles of classical architecture.

THE LINEAR HOUSE

The history of the vernacular, linear house goes back to at least 1600, but its true origins may well be lost in the mists of the distant past, with the raths and crannog dwellings of ancient Celtic society, and perhaps even earlier. Rectangular in plan, it is never more than one room deep, the depth of that one room (usually between twelve and fifteen feet) being determined by the length of the roof timbers which were available. Thus it may grow in length and sometimes in height, but never in depth. It evolved slowly through time up to the latter half of the nineteenth century. In its most common form it has three compartments with the kitchen, the most important room, placed centrally between two bedrooms. Food was prepared on the hearth over a fire which was usually at floor level, and which was never allowed to go out, being rekindled each morning from a glowing ember. In the evening, when work was done, neighbours would gather in the kitchen to entertain each other with music, dancing and story telling.

A smaller version has only two rooms, a kitchen and bedroom, with the sleeping accommodation set against the hearth wall and warmed by it. Within this extremely simple plan surprising variety was achieved with different roof types and building materials, and even in the internal layout and positioning of the hearth. And of course each cottage was part of its own particular landscape with its own arrangement of outbuildings, boundaries, entrance piers and gates.

Smaller again was the cottage in its most basic form: a humble one-room dwelling that was sometimes shared by the animals. This used to be a common practice throughout north-western Europe, for cattle were a valuable asset, and it was essential to be able to attend to them easily, particularly during bad winter weather. Irish 'byre houses', common in north-western and western parts of the country, were built on a slope, the lower end being reserved for the animals, with a drain to discharge effluent away from the upper end, which was for living. If fortunes improved the family would build a separate byre, usually attached to the house, and convert the animal area for their own use. They might also make a loft over part of the ground floor, reached by a ladder or stairs from the kitchen, which they would use as a bedroom or, divided in half, as two bedrooms. The space was lit by a small window in the gable (gable windows were never used on the ground floor). The ceilings of both the kitchen and the loft were open to, and followed the slope of, the roof.

Roofs are gabled in the north-west and west. Here it is not uncommon for such cottages to have two doors opening directly into the kitchen (on the side away from the hearth) on opposite sides of the house: the inhabitants would choose which one to use according to the direction from which the wind was blowing. The front door incorporated a half-door, useful for keeping animals out and children in. It also allowed more light into the kitchen, helped the draught for the fire and provided a convenient support to lean on when chatting to neighbours or passers by. A superstition attached to the use of the back door, for according to Estyn Evans in Irish Heritage 'the stranger must never be allowed to leave the house this way lest he take the luck of the house with him'.

In these gabled houses there was sometimes a 'nook', or bed outshot (alcove), close to the hearth, big enough to take a double bed, for the use of the senior members of the household, without encroaching on the important space around the hearth. A curtain (replacing the earlier woven wicker screen) was hung in front to screen the bed from view.

Moving towards the midlands, eastern and southern areas, roofs become half-hipped and hipped, and the entrance (here there is usually only one door, to the front) is positioned in line with the hearth. A screen wall was built in front of the entrance to protect the interior from view, and sometimes incorporated a little window through which the dweller could see who might be calling. These houses are often larger than their northern gabled counterparts, and include sleeping lofts over the entire ground floor.

Walls are invariably of solid construction, and are usually of stone, though mud was used where stone was scarce – often on the better land in the midlands, east and south-east. Both stone and mud walls were often lime-rendered both inside and out. Sometimes the stone was just limewashed, and the layers have built up over many years to give a smooth, undulating surface which seems to echo the landscape. All over Donegal limewashed houses still vie with each other in their crisp, gleaming whiteness, though nowadays, unfortunately, modern paints take the place of traditional limewash.

The home of a typical small farmer, whose holding was often only a few acres subleased from other tenant farmers or determined by subdivision of land as it passed from father to sons, differed little from the cottages of rural labourers, carpenters or blacksmiths. Ulster weavers' cottages, with their attached work rooms, were also similar, though the cottages of country crafts people were more than mere shops: they were important meeting places where people dallied and exchanged news. Migrant country dwellers, on the other hand, constantly on the move in search of work, would build temporary one-room cabins of sod, simply abandoning them when the time came to leave. Such cottages dotted the countryside prior to the famine years of the 1840s, but few have survived. An attractive example can be seen at Ferns in Co. Wexford, built of stone and limewashed. Traditionally roofs were thatched, but later many were replaced with iron or slates. Roofs were always pitched, with the chimney stack on the ridge. Sometimes a second chimney was added for visual balance, but served no practical function. Occasionally the main roof would extend out to cover a little porch, sometimes called a windbreak, or the porch would have its own separate roof.

A number of houses were extended upwards to provide a second storey over either the entire area of the house or just part of it, as in the American President Woodrow Wilson's ancestral homestead at Dergalt, Strabane. Many two-storey houses throughout the country grew from single-storey cottages in the late nineteenth and early twentieth centuries, when grants were available to cover most of the cost. Very often the roof covering was also changed from thatch to slate, which was more easily maintained, and outbuildings were also recovered with slate or more commonly, corrugated iron. Thatching continued to be used in some areas, however, especially those where slate was not easily available.

The people who lived in these cottages were not concerned with being 'different': the rules were understood and adhered to, and the dwellings consequently seem to grow out of the soil and to belong. It is difficult to date these houses. Many were built during the eighteenth and nineteenth centuries, often possibly on earlier foundations which may go back to medieval times. The outbuildings were usually added later; on larger farms, barns were built from the mid-eighteenth to the mid-nineteenth century, when corn growing became important.

A number of early examples of full two-storey thatched houses, known as 'thatched mansions', still survive, such as the one at Clearistown, Co. Wexford, now a post office. A few other surviving houses can be dated to the seventeenth and early eighteenth centuries: these tended to be the substantial homes of well-to-do farmers, which often combined both vernacular and formal features. Many were replaced during the eighteenth century by Georgian style houses.

In the unsettled times before the seventeenth century, buildings were constructed with defence in mind. In the country this gave rise to the tower houses: structures with the rooms piled one above the other, with living quarters on upper floors. Many of these houses still remain in a ruinous state, though some have been restored and are lived in again. During the first decades of the seventeenth century, at the time of the Ulster Plantations, the new landowners were required to build their houses within protective walls. Stone and brick were the preferred materials, with slate for roofs, and two floors were considered better than one. Many prefabricated timber-frame houses were also built, however, and the simple mud house with a thatched roof persisted, despite the earnest hope of the new arrivals that their superior influence might encourage the native Irish to upgrade the standard of their cottages.

CLASSICAL STYLES

Classical styles, revived and favoured by Italian architects of the fifteenth century, developed by Palladio in the sixteenth century, and gradually adopted throughout Europe, eventually arrived in Ireland three centuries later. The timing was extremely apposite, for during the peaceful years of the eighteenth century landlords set about investing in their residences, either by remodelling and adding to existing houses or by building new ones and developing their estates. Classical and Palladian principles were applied to many fine new stately houses, and in time their influence filtered down to the builders of more humble homes.

This trend was largely disseminated through 'pattern' books like Richard Morrison's *Useful and Ornamental Designs in Architecture (Villas)* ... (1793) which included designs for 'The Parsonage or Small Farmhouse' – a simple box, two storeys high and three bays wide – as well as for 'The Villa or Hunting Lodge' and (at the top of the scale) 'A Temporary Residence for a Gentleman whose Principal Residence is in England'.

Such house designs were intended to be practical and convenient for modern living, and were a revolutionary alternative to linear development, which hitherto had been the accepted way to add extra rooms. Instead of entering directly into the kitchen, which was now given a secondary position, the main entrance led into a hall, from which each room could be entered separately. The servants, who in the linear house often slept in lofts over outbuildings, were now accommodated under the same roof as the family. And – of no small importance – they were fashionable, being scaled-down versions of the more important big houses. Their popularity was assured, and designs based on them were used to replace many of the earlier thatched mansions and tower houses in every part of the country.

Such houses might be of two storeys, or of two or three over a basement. The stairway is either in the front hallway or to the rear, where it is lit by a tall round-headed window. Windows have up-and-down sliding sashes divided into a number of panes and the frames are of timber. Entrance doors, placed centrally in the facade, are panelled and have fanlights over. Externally the walls are usually rendered and sometimes painted. Roofs are slated and at times hipped. The relationship of all the elements to each other and to the whole is one of harmonious proportion.

Modified versions were built by tenant farmers on estates, the house varying in scale according to the size of the farm. Many are simple two-storey houses, three bays wide and with little if any adornment on their facades. Interior decoration is generally simple, with plain undecorated plasterwork. Their farmyards, which are mostly attached, are of varying arrangements. Houses such as these continued to be built right through the nineteenth century and up to the 1950s. With their entrances and driveways and mature surrounding landscape they contribute considerably to the

CARLINGFORD, Co. Louth

Nestling at the foot of Carlingford Mountain and looking out over Carlingford Lough to the Mourne Mountains in Co. Down, the small town of Carlingford is like a city in miniature. It has a medieval street plan with a number of important small-scale medieval buildings: the Tholsel, the Mint, Taffe's Castle and, most impressive, Carlingford Castle on its strategic site commanding the harbour. Its streets, however, are lined mainly with buildings from the eighteenth and nineteenth centuries: houses big and small, shops, hostelries, public buildings and religious establishments. Small houses and cottages make a large contribution to its character. There are charming lime-rendered whitewashed cottages of one and two-storeys and slate-roofed houses with smooth plastered façades and plaster details gloss-painted in attractive colour schemes.

beauty of the Irish countryside. Vernacular houses, not to be totally outdone, were also to adopt panelled doorways with fanlights overhead and windows of classical influence in their strenuous, if modest, efforts to keep up with the fashion of the day.

The classical influence was equally strong in towns: many cottages built during this period display a concern for balance and symmetry in a variety of ways, while great care is taken to introduce interest in the arrangement of windows and doors. Adjacent houses in terraces sometimes have paired doorways, often detailed. as a unified design: there are charming examples of them in Newry, where in more substantial terraces a carriage arch is included between the doorways, and in Kilkenny city. Many are rendered in plaster and painted; simple and without ornament though they may be, they are unmistakably classical in essence.

NEAR ANTRIM TOWN,
Co. Antrim

Visitors to such a cottage as this would be invited to sit by the hearth on a low stool or stone slab built into the fireplace, for this is the social centre of the home, the place for entertainment, 'ceili' and meeting. Here a pot of food is cooking on a turf fire. Bread was baked in bastable pots, which are made of cast iron and have a lid; other food was prepared in three-legged pots and griddles over the open fire, and cast-iron kettles were used to boil water. The fire is surrounded by stone flags and is usually at ground level. Traditionally, it rarely died out, there always being a burning ember left with which to rekindle it each morning.

STRABANE,
Co. Tyrone

This interesting example of a linear house which has been extended and partly raised was the home of the grandfather of United States President Woodrow Wilson. Soundly built of local stone, limewashed and thatched with flax, which lasts up to twenty years, it illustrates both continuity and progression. An extended raised section breaks through the roof of the earlier single-storey home to give first-floor accommodation under a new slate roof. The slate-roofed stable attached to the upper end of the house may have been added at the same time. At the lower end is the byre, the most important of the outbuildings, which also include (out of the picture) pigsties, a cart shed and a small store, all thatched in straw. Sensitively restored and administered by the National Trust in Northern Ireland, it is now in the ownership of the Northern Ireland Government.

MALIN HEAD,
Co. Donegal

This farm complex is situated on inhospitable stony ground on Malin Head, the most northerly part of the country and very much a place of its own. The buildings are informally grouped, having been added at different stages and create a vague sense of enclosure. The house is the oldest building and the two-storey barn to the right the newest, added by a progressive member of the family in the 1930s. Despite their different roofing material — thatch on the house, iron and slate on the outbuildings — the buildings are united by the matching proportions of their windows, doors and roof pitches and by the use of stone and limewash throughout.

URRIS HILLS,
Co. Donegal

This thatched two-room cottage in the Urris Hills overlooking Lough Swilly has a small porch, over which the main roof extends, and attached outbuildings of lower roof height. These have a different roof covering and were probably added later, but they continue the line of the house, all following the slope of the ground and the flow of the hill. Sensibly, they shelter against the side of the hill, which offers protection from winds in this peaty mountainous area.

MEENACLADY,
Co. Donegal

The extended house can sometimes go on almost forever: dwelling, byre and hayloft, stable, dairy, store, piggery and on and on, all linked together in one line. The term 'long house' could not be more appropriate for this example from Donegal. Each unit of the building is defined by the cross-walls rising to gables above roof level. The only two-storey section contains a hayloft on the upper level with an external stairway leading to it. The group would have developed informally and without any specific plan. It has an urban quality, and the yard which runs along the front of such buildings was often referred to as 'the street'.

NEAR DUNFANAGHY,
Co. Donegal

*Here the main house has been
extended in line to incorporate a
range of outbuildings, each
indicating the progress and
development of the farm. The
dwelling is thatched and has four
windows to the rear, the lit one
being in the kitchen, from where the
left-hand chimney rises from the
hearth. Emanating a cosy warmth,
the house stands out softly with its
limewashed walls against the
backdrop of a dull cloudy evening
sky. Hay stacks are ready for
removal to the barn.*

HORN HEAD,
Co. Donegal

*Each section of this linear-type
house can be observed from the
cross walls extending above roof
level. The roofs of the dwelling area
are slated while those of the
outbuildings are of corrugated iron.
Windows have sliding up-and-
down sashes, each with three panes,
and the doors are timber sheeted. A
low sky of threatening grey clouds
accentuates the whiteness of the
limewashed walls, against which the
painted doors and the green
foreground provide a striking and
colourful contrast.*

ERRIGAL,
Co. Donegal

Dramatically situated beneath Errigal, a cone-shaped quartzite mountain and the highest peak in Donegal, these cottages look quite tiny in comparison. Nevertheless they boldly assert their presence, standing out crisp and white in the surrounding oasis of green fields. The group in the foreground is of the extended, linear, gabled type with slated roof and chimney stacks on the ridge. Just beyond it, behind the trees, a more recent house can be seen.

MAGHERAROARTY,
Co. Donegal

This farmhouse, viewed here from behind, has attached outbuildings in linear fashion with a small lean-to built onto the right-hand gable and a separate outbuilding to the left at right angles to the main buildings. The roofs are both thatched and slated. The little window (rear windows were unusual in these houses) lights the kitchen from where the chimney appears on the ridge. The garden in the foreground is cultivated with a good potato crop. The hay has been saved, and the last touches are being made to the stacks in readiness for feeding the cattle through the winter.

NEAR
LETTERMACAWARD,
Co. Donegal

This two-room house with central doorway is set in a textured landscape of rocks, shallow pockets of earth and tufted grass near Gweebarra Bay. One or two scrawny trees have taken root together with a few small shrubs. Wild fuschias, which make colourful hedgerows in many coastal areas, bloom in the left foreground. The atmosphere, while aesthetically pleasing, indicates an unyielding earth and a hard life for the occupiers.

NEAR GLENTIES,
Co. Donegal

A small thatched roadside farmhouse of the typical Donegal gabled variety is reached by a narrow country boreen, away from busy traffic routes. Little landscaping, except for a few trees, marks its presence. The small area of ploughed field and the single haystack in the middle distance indicate the limited opportunities for agriculture and point to a simple way of life.

NEAR WESTPORT,
Co. Mayo

A three-room dwelling with central kitchen, as indicated by the chimney, slate roof and raised gables, this cottage has two little gabled outbuildings stepped down in height which continue the long building line. Tucked into a rocky slope, it is dwarfed by the great peak of Croagh Patrick. Every year pilgrims flock here to make the gruelling ascent to the summit — and the even more slippery descent. Now gold has been discovered in this unlikely spot and its remote beauty is under threat.

INISHBOFIN,
Co. Galway

The island of Inishbofin, in the Atlantic off the Connemara coast of north Galway, has a long history of habitation. Population numbers have fluctuated over the years and there has been continuing emigration. The main source of income was traditionally fishing, followed by farming. Turf cut from the bogs provided fuel. These houses of the western vernacular type originally had roofs thatched with straw, now largely replaced by slates. Windows were small and on front elevations only. There were two entrance doors, both leading straight into the kitchen, one to the front and one to the rear. Kitchen floors were of beaten earth, and many bedroom floors would have been of timber. The islanders lived simple lives, and their furniture (which would have included a spinning wheel, since they wore homespun clothing) would have been basic.

NEAR BALLYCONNEELY,
Co. Galway

The very practical half-door was common to many smaller linear houses. It allows in extra light and air during the day, at the same time keeping animals out and children in. It is also useful for leaning on when chatting to passers-by. In gabled houses, which often had an entrance door back and front, the front door usually had the half-door, which was in fact a secondary door fixed to the outside of the same opening. Both doors would commonly be made of deal and open inwards.

LETTERMORE,
Co. Galway

The unassuming charm of this cottage is greatly enhanced by its neatly cultivated vegetable patch, used principally in the past for growing the potatoes on which life in rural Ireland depended. The 'lazy-beds' of this system were used extensively in the west: furrows were cut and the sod turned upside down on to the ridges so that the decomposing grass could feed the crop. The width of furrows, sometimes up to 3 ft (0.9 m), depended on the quality and depth of soil, and the ridges also varied in width from 2 ft (0.6 m) to 4 ft (1.2 m). A plot like this would provide a family with vegetables for most of the year. The dry-stone boundary wall is neatly executed, and in the usual fashion has larger stones at its base and smaller on top. Sometimes chimneys were added for visual balance rather than for use, so it may be that there is only one working chimney here, serving the kitchen hearth.

KILTOOM,
Co. Roscommon

This three-room gabled and thatched cottage in Co. Roscommon is presented with a fierce pride. It is the home of Mrs Leonard, who says it is one hundred years old, and certainly its appearance cannot have changed much since the nineteenth century. Inside, it consists of a kitchen with original hearth, a parlour and a bedroom; outside it still has its small windows and thatched roof, and its outbuildings, painted red and white, are situated on the other side of the road.

One room leads directly into another without a separating passageway. Here the parlour, traditionally used only on special occasions, is entered directly from the kitchen.

BURREN,
Co. Clare

This house makes a simple stark statement in its Atlantic coast setting, with no outbuildings, planting or protective slope to shield it from the prevailing wind. A line of stone wall, punctuated by a blue gate, appears to hold it in place only metres away from the edge. Stone-built, rendered and whitewashed, with a typical grey slate roof, this three-room cottage turns its back to the sea, giving no clue to any means of livelihood which might support its owner.

NEAR MILLTOWN
MALBAY,
Co. Clare

A small, whitewashed, three-roomed, stone cottage backs onto Liscannor Bay and the Atlantic Ocean. Its gabled roof is thatched and tied down with rope at the eaves. The single chimney indicates the position of the hearth, and the entrance door leads directly into the kitchen. The little lean-to outbuilding was probably added later. Beside it haystacks have been prepared for the winter-feeding of cattle. The direction of the prevailing wind is clearly marked by the direction in which the stunted bushes are growing.

NEAR ADARE,
Co. Limerick

Hearth-lobby houses such as this are typical of central, eastern and south-eastern areas. A screen wall shields the kitchen from view when the door is open, and the hearth is in line with the entrance, as indicated by the position of the single chimney. The roof, steeply pitched with hipped ends, is covered with straw thatch – now becoming harder to replace because of modern harvesting methods and new strains of wheat with shorter stems. A porch, created from a small projection, is also included under the main roof cover. The windows have small panes and up-and-down sliding sashes, and their proportions suit not only the building and the climate, but also the needs of the occupiers, as they leave areas of wall space free for other uses internally. The pale yellow wash, not uncommon to this part of the country, gives added warmth to the building.

NEAR CROOM,
Co. Limerick

This cottage has a steeply pitched thatched and hipped roof over three compartments, with four-paned sliding sash windows and a doorway with a top panel glazed in small panes. It is rendered and washed in the warm cream colour often to be seen in this area. Two small square piers with sloping caps define its entrance, which is through a wrought-iron gate, and a neat hedge of privet surrounds the garden which, like the cottage, is evidently a source of pleasure and pride to those who live here.

NEAR NEWPORT,
Co. Tipperary

Tower houses were built during turbulent periods from the thirteenth century right up to the seventeenth century. Primarily defensive in purpose with their living accommodation at the top, they were influenced in their architecture by Norman ideas of castle building. Indeed, they were commonly called castles and were striking features of the landscape, particularly in Counties Cork, Clare, Galway, Tipperary and Limerick. Built to the highest standards of craftsmanship, they have endured centuries of neglect. As they were too strong to demolish when they were abandoned, some of their stones have been cannibalized for use in later buildings. Despite this and the ravages of the weather, many still stand, albeit in a ruinous state. A number have been restored and renovated for modern use, the most famous being Thor Balylee in Co. Sligo, owned by William Butler Yeats.

NEAR NEWTOWN SANDES,
Co. Kerry

Painted classical details – quoins, a vague suggestion of columns, pediments over windows, a plinth and a band under the eaves – lend this otherwise simple vernacular house a touch of eccentric and rather whimsical grandeur. The straw thatch roof is hipped, with sloping ends, and is fixed down at the ridge with rows of scallops. This type of roof, not so well equipped as others to withstand storms and gales, is common in the midlands and south-east.

NEAR MYROSS,
Co. Cork

This house, on one of the many pretty inlets on the Cork coastline, is of delightfully simple expression and composition, partly two-storey and partly single-storey, with steeply pitched slate roofs and gables rising above roof level. The Cork coast, with its gentle climate warmed by the Gulf Stream, has always been a popular place for building. Many small towns and villages have developed around its attractive harbours.

Dwyer MacAllister Cottage
GLEN OF IMAAL,
Co. Wicklow

Dwyer MacAllister Cottage has been preserved because of its associations with Michael Dwyer, a famous rebel who was trapped here by the English in 1799. Another member of his group, Samuel MacAllister, saved Dwyer's life by acting as a decoy, sacrificing his life so that Dwyer could escape. Furnished in a traditional manner, the cottage is an interesting example of the vernacular style. It is in the care of the Office of Public Works and is open to the public.

OLD LEIGHLIN,
Co. Carlow

Combined dwellings and post offices are to be found throughout Ireland, and the postmaster or mistress is probably about the best-known individual in any community. Generally such premises are kept very neatly and look more like houses than businesses. Discreet signs are adequate to identify their function as post offices. The simple beauty of this one at Old Leighlin stems from its charming proportions, neat appearance and freedom from unnecessary signs.

RIDGE,
Co. Carlow

During the late nineteenth and early twentieth centuries, grants were made available to improve existing cottages and farmhouses. Many single-storey thatched cottages were extended; first floors were added, sometimes over part of the existing house and sometimes over the entire ground floor; outbuildings were erected; and thatch roofing was replaced with corrugated iron or slates. It is likely that this house at Ridge in Co. Carlow was originally a single-storey house with the first floor and a new slate roof added over the entire existing building and the chimney stack built up in brick. Nevertheless, it retains its appealing vernacular character.

KILMORE QUAY,
Co. Wexford

The fishing village of Kilmore Quay consists of a long informal street wandering southwards to the sea and lined with whitewashed thatched cottages. Some cottages are single-storey and some one-and-a-half-storey, some have half-hipped gables and others dormer windows, but all are whitewashed, with gate piers and low planting at the base of the walls, and are neat, crisp and extremely picturesque. Just off the coast of Kilmore are the Saltee Islands, now a bird sanctuary and formerly home to late Stone Age settlers, Christian hermits, monks, pirates and smugglers. To the west, across Ballytiege Bay is the Hook lighthouse, 750 years old and possibly the oldest in Europe. As early as the fifth century the monks kept a fire lit there to warn passing vessels.

FERNS,
Co. Wexford

In the past a typical poor labourer's cottage would have consisted of just one room. In lieu of rent the labourer would work for the farmer, on whose land it stood, for an agreed number of days. With the cottage he would have a small patch of ground on which to grow vegetables and keep some poultry to support his family. If he was lucky he would have secure employment from the farmer, and his wife might also be employed to do the housework. The less fortunate would move from place to place, abandoning cottage after cottage in search of work. Many such cottages were built of sods and would have no luxuries. The single room would contain a simple hearth and basic furniture on a beaten earth floor. This house, although the remnant of a once larger one built sturdily of stone, gives a good impression of what such a simple house would have appeared like.

CLEARISTOWN,
Co. Wexford

Viewed across the cemetery, this early two-storey house, now the post office, is an example of what is often referred to as a 'thatched mansion'. Such houses, dating from the late seventeenth and early eighteenth centuries, were the homes of comfortable farmers, and many were replaced by the more fashionable classical box houses of the eighteenth and nineteenth centuries. Fortunately a few survive. The present owners of this house say it is three hundred years old and that it has been in their family for over a century.

BALLAGHKEEN,
Co. Wexford

In Wexford the traditional cottage/farmhouse has a hipped and thatched roof which is usually steeply pitched. The hearth is invariably in line with the entrance lobby, which has a screen wall to protect the kitchen's privacy. Here the rooms contained in lofts within the roof space are reached by pull-down ladders at each end of the kitchen. Wexford has made efforts to protect its traditional cottages and farmhouses, by providing small grants, for instance, for the maintenance of thatched roofs.

MULLAGH,
Co. Cavan

The Church of Ireland was engaged
in a good deal of house building
during the first decades of the
nineteenth century, when glebe
houses were built throughout the
country assisted by government
funding. Many were designed by
John Bowden, architect to the
Board of First Fruits, which was
responsible for church building.
Glebe houses are characteristic of
the period in which they were built:
influenced by current fashions, they
in turn must have had an effect on
the architecture of many
contemporary and later farmhouse
buildings. This glebe house, on the
shores of Mullagh lake in Co.
Cavan, is typical of the type. Two
storeys high, with a three-bay
pleasantly proportioned façade, it
has a slated and hipped roof and a
pair of chimney stacks. Painted in
its original deep terracotta and
surrounded by a mature landscape,
it successfully conveys the immense
charm of such houses.

NEAR LETTERKENNY,
Co. Donegal

In an otherwise mountainous and
rugged county, Letterkenny, the
county town of Donegal, lies in a
sheltered oasis of lush green. This
substantial farmhouse with
attached outhouses is very different
from the typical Donegal farms and
cottages, which tend to be smaller,
linear and situated on windswept
rocky hillsides. Sitting on its
prosperous holding against a
background of mature tress, the five
bay, two-storey buildings painted
in white and red are freshly
presented and impressive in scale.

NEAR KILCULLEN,
Co. Kildare

*'Convenience, strength,
commodiousness and beauty and
this art (to make all buildings so) is
called architecture', states Richard
Morrison in the introduction to his
Useful and Ornamental
Designs in Architecture
(1793). Certainly, the classical box
house, which he among other
eighteenth- and nineteenth-century
architects must take a share of
credit for popularizing, has all these
attributes. It is of simple and
unornamented style, and of
pleasing and harmonious
proportions. In the midst of
excellent quality farming land, this
example of a box house from Co.
Kildare has a projecting gabled
porch, the only protrusion in an
otherwise unassuming façade, and
perhaps a later addition. Two
monkey puzzle trees at the entrance
frame the house and lead in to the
garden, now neglected and
becoming overgrown, for the house
is sadly without occupant.*

CLONSILLA,
Co. Kildare

*As the fashion for classical designs
was taken up throughout the
country and modified, the style
became simplified down to its
essentials, and examples were built
with little or no architectural
features. Often described as 'box'
houses, these houses have balanced
façades and central doorways, and
are square or rectangular in plan,
of two storeys and with slated roofs,
often hipped and with one or two
chimney stacks. They are usually
built of stone and plaster-rendered.
This example from Clonsilla has the
added attractions of mature
landscaping and delightfully simple
railings.*

CARNEW,
Co. Wicklow

In town building the integrity of the street line is all important. Where access to the rear of buildings was needed, it was provided in many towns and villages by means of arched openings between buildings. The arches are virtually always built over a first-floor level, thus maintaining the street line. This street at Carnew is in simple classical style, rendered and painted. Here the arched rear access is the centre of a balanced design which includes the entrance doorway to houses at each side.

CASTLECOMER,
Co. Kilkenny

In the past shopkeepers generally lived over the shop. The shop-cum-dwelling is a typical example: a separate doorway leads to the living accommodation on the upper floor, and the shopfront, of classical inspiration, is simply and attractively designed with a hand-painted fascia. The solid gate to the left leads to the rear of the building. This is just one of the many impressive buildings which, together with the tree-lined main street, gives Castlecomer its attractive and pleasing character.

KILTEGAN,
Co. Wicklow

Kiltegan is an attractive small village which was attached to the Humewood Castle Estate off the Dublin-to-Baltinglass road just a few miles from Baltinglass. It has a village green, terraced estate cottages and a charming church approached by a long driveway leading to it from the village. Called 'Felicity', this is a pleasantly proportioned two-storey house finished with a rough-cast render. It has attractive window and door surrounds, a pitched and gabled roof with chimney stacks at each end, a stone wall to the side and an open gravelled forecourt. The entrance door leads in to a central hall which has rooms off it to each side. Neatly presented, it contributes in no small way to the varied charm of Kiltegan.

DUNNAMAGGAN,
Co. Kilkenny

Built in 1840 in miniature Palladian style, this delightful house – called Loughbrack Cottage – has a two-storey, three-bay section and a single-storey wing to each side. It was the generous gift of the owners of Ballaghtobin House to a young woman in their employment who married a member of the local constabulary (the local barracks still stand virtually next door). It was later occupied by a Mr Sherwood, a steward employed by the Gabbeth family, new owners of the estate, and stayed in the Sherwood family until a few years ago. The cottage was originally one room deep, with central stairs leading to upper floors and has been carefully enlarged by its present owners, who have incorporated a lean-to outbuilding to the rear. Happily, the house, with its pretty gardens, retains all its original charm.

Location and Building Materials

MACGILLYCUDDYS
REEKS,
Co. Kerry

Macgillycuddys Reeks in Co. Kerry contain Carrantuohill, the highest peak in the country. The pattern of small to medium-size fields stretches as far as possible into the foothills, where the distinction between the responsive workable land and the unconquerable becomes evident. The fields are bounded by hedges, and surround a number of medium-size farm complexes. Farming here is mainly dairy, and holdings would traditionally have consisted of approximately 50 acres or more (20 hectares).

In a country untouched by the Industrial Revolution, where farming was traditionally the main source of livelihood, to a large degree the quality of the land dictated life styles, which in turn were reflected in the dwellings. The nature of the land varies from unproductive mountains and boglands, through the poor, shallow soil of Co. Leitrim and the Drumlin Hills of Co. Cavan, to the rich, fertile land of the midlands and south-east. Shaped like a dish, Ireland has mountains around its perimeter in coastal areas and a lowland central plain. The west coast endures the first force of the prevailing winds which blow in from the Atlantic, laden with rain. The east and south-east coasts, facing England, Europe and the Irish Sea, are drier. These general climatic conditions have always influenced the choice of both site and building methods for Irish cottages.

Traditional builders used whatever materials were to hand – local materials were used for all but the most important buildings – and so their buildings seem totally at home in the landscape. Vernacular styles, never formally designed, were built with skills learned and passed on from one generation to the next. New styles, such as the box type or classical house, based on eighteenth-century influences and the pattern-book designs of the eighteenth and early nineteenth centuries, were similarly taken on board by local craftsmen and assimilated into their methods.

In the coastal areas fishermen's cottages are of the simple vernacular type. Little but the upturned curragh and fishing nets sets them apart from other dwellings. In the foothills of mountains, where the land is cultivated within clearly defined boundaries, are little farms of simple construction, with outbuildings added according to the suitability of the site rather than any formal plan. In the midlands, east and the south-east farmhouses are large. Many are two-storey and in the classical style, plaster-rendered and painted. Some are of two and three storeys over a basement. Often they have decorative details in the form of moulded door and window surrounds, and raised quoins painted in contrasting colours. There are also, particularly in Co. Wexford and elsewhere in the midlands, houses in the vernacular style which are equally substantial. Farms in this part of the country often have impressive courtyards. Ireland's many rivers, canals and lakes created their own settings for the many cottages which grew up alongside them. Lock-keepers' houses were scenes of great activity, while turf-cutters' cottages and large country houses alike drew peace and serenity, as well as material resources, from the lakes and rivers they overlooked.

In towns cottages were built in single-storey and two-storey terraces, often finished in plaster, but sometimes of stone or stone with brick trim, as in Cahir and Tipperary town, or of brick, as in Castlecomer, Co. Kilkenny and in Dublin city. Many of these were built with slate roofs, but earlier town cottages would originally have been thatched and were re-roofed in slate during the nineteenth century, when slates – which were easier to erect and proved more lasting – became more easily available.

House-builders on exposed north-west and west coast areas built gabled houses with round ridged thatched roofs, often of marram grasses with an under-roof of sods. Other materials used for thatching were flax, the waste from flax scutching, straw, reeds, bracken, potato haulm and even heather. In order to give a rounded ridge the principal rafter trusses did not meet at the ridge but were joined by a horizontal member on which the ridge member rests. Roofs were tied down with a network of ropes, secured at the eaves by being tied to pegs built into the wall, or weighted with loose stones which hang below or above the eaves. Generally a lath was fixed across the eaves to prevent ropes cutting into the thatch. In some places, for instance in Co. Mayo, ropes were carried horizontally across stepped gables and tied at gable ends. Such methods developed out of respect for the winds which reach gale force for at least thirty days annually.

In the midlands and south-east more clement conditions allow for a different approach. The roofs here are mostly steeply pitched and often incorporate an entire second floor lit by dormer windows. They are half-hipped or hipped, and thatched usually by the scallop- or thrust-thatching method, using straw of wheat, rye or oats collected at harvest time, or reeds collected from riversides. The thatcher was a skilled craftsman: when his work was carefully done, thatch of wheat or rye would have a life of up to twelve years. Scallop thatching involves fixing the thatch to the roof using 'scallops', or wooden rods, while in thrust thatching the ear end of a layer of thatch is twisted into a knot and thrust tightly into another layer. When the roof is covered with overlapping layers, the ridge is secured with a clay or concrete coping, or sometimes with a ridge board of wood or sheet iron.

Slates were used as a roofing material from the eighteenth century and earlier, but it was during the nineteenth century that their use became more widespread, and now they are the most common type of roofing to be seen throughout the island. Prepared at local quarries, they range in texture from coarse and heavy, as in Co. Clare, to smooth and light, as on Valencia Island in Co. Kerry, and in colour from the greys and green-greys of Co. Clare and west Cork to the blue-blacks of Valencia Island. They were also imported from the Welsh quarries, and slates such as Blue Bangors became a very competitive and much-used alternative to local slates.

Impermeable, light, long-lasting, versatile and aesthetically pleasing, slates have many desirable qualities. They were also used for sills, damp-proof courses, paving and, in exposed areas, cladding walls. The main problem with old slate roofs is the manner in which they were fixed, since the iron nails corrode and become insecure. In recent decades, asbestos slates have been widely used as a cheaper substitute, but there are indications that slates are once again being recognized as a superior material and the demand for quarried slates is growing.

Towards the end of the nineteenth century corrugated iron became available in long lengths. Light and easily worked, it was a tempting replacement for thatch. Some cottages were completely clad with it and look quite charming, but it requires regular painting and can look ugly if neglected. Roofing tiles were also unusual until the late nineteenth century, when tile-making improved. Baked tiles were followed by concrete tiles, which, being less expensive than slate, became popular in the 1930s and 1940s for domestic buildings.

External walls, supporting the roofs, were universally of mass construction, of stone or mud, frequently lime-rendered and washed. More recently, from the beginning of this century, concrete has been used, first in mass form, like mud, and later in blocks, like masonry. Aesthetically unacceptable as a finish, it is usually plastered over with sand and cement. In vernacular building internal walls were of wattle, or sometimes a piece of furniture such as a dresser acted as a dividing wall. Stone was used in more substantial houses, and more recently concrete blocks and timber stud partitions have appeared.

Archaeological evidence points to the early use of timber-framed construction, although no examples now exist. Depletion of the forest for commercial purposes in the sixteenth and seventeenth centuries ensured the end of any tradition which may have existed. The Ulster Plantations of 1609 saw the importation of timber-frame styles from England, however, as can be seen illustrated by Thomas Raven in Sir Thomas Phillips' survey of the Londonderry plantation in 1622, but the last examples disappeared in the beginning of the nineteenth century.

Stone is traditionally the most commonly used building material throughout the island. The most widespread form is limestone, which constitutes the entire central area of the country and parts of the west, such as Counties Clare and Sligo. This beautiful stone, sometimes a shining blue-black colour, as in Kilkenny, is used not only for walls, but also for details, gate piers and paving flags, and being softer than granite it is also used for decorative work. Granite, the most durable of stones and another important building material, is native to such counties as Wicklow, Carlow, Dublin, Galway, Down, Donegal and Antrim. In the south and south-west the local stone is old red sandstone: beautifully varied in colour, it can be seen in buildings throughout west Cork and also in parts of Ulster.

In the stony north-western and western areas of the country, where every small pocket of soil was valuable, stones cleared from the fields were used both for buildings and for field boundaries. Usually the stones were laid in courses, but sometimes not, and were lime-rendered or coated with limewash, which over the years built up a protective surface. The best stones of good size were kept for quoins, where strength is important, and cut stones, when used, were confined to details such as window sills and window and door surrounds. Such cottages can be seen along the west coast, from Donegal to west Cork: fresh and white, with small stone outbuildings, they are an inseparable part of the landscape.

Sometimes the stonework was bonded with dry mortar, and sometimes it was simply drybuilt. In areas where lime was available lime mortar was used: as transportation became easier in the eighteenth and nineteenth centuries lime became more widely available, but because of cost it would generally only have been used for the houses of the better off, and certainly not for those of the landless poor.

Ashlar stonework was never used in vernacular building but in the early nineteenth century the estates built a number of cottages and whole villages, such as Ardagh in Co. Longford, Fenagh in Co. Carlow and Shillelagh in Co. Wicklow, using good quality stonework of limestone, granite or sandstone. Later in the century the public authorities continued their example as, for instance, at Castledermot, Co. Carlow, and near Athy, Co. Kildare. Striking black basalt from the Antrim plateau was used mainly in east Co. Derry and in Co. Antrim, where there is a fine example at Clonavon Street in Ballymena.

The mud used in the midlands and south-east was not, as might at first be thought, an inferior or intrinsically poor building material. The mud was layered with straw, each layer being allowed to dry before the next was placed. As the soil was good and the climate relatively dry, mud was more suitable here than elsewhere, particularly when built on a few courses of stone, and because of its insulating properties it made for warm and cosy cottages. Mud cottages are to be found in both town and country. Now often abandoned, these beautifully soft buildings are sadly unappreciated and rarely restored.

Sods, the most readily available material of all, were commonly used for the cottages of the poor and of landless labourers. A house of sods, cut and laid like blocks, could be erected in twenty-four hours, a valuable advantage for a population ever on the move in search of work. Few if any examples remain today.

As external walls tended to be rendered throughout the country, it is difficult to tell at a glance the material beneath. However it is only too easy to tell the difference between natural materials and concrete, for while the former appears soft and pleasing, the latter is rigid and angular.

Limewash, one of the commonest external finishes, was often left white, but sometimes pigments were added to give a variety of attractive colours, yellow ochre being among the most popular. A tradition for the use of colour (now mostly achieved with paint) developed throughout the country, most notably in the towns of the south of Ireland and in west Cork.

Lime plaster was another popular traditional finish. This was built up in two or three layers, and rough cast was achieved by flicking small pebbles from a hawk on to the wet final coat. From the nineteenth century Portland cement, was used to strengthen plaster, which at times was lined to simulate stonework, an effect to be seen on many seaside cottages. Smooth plaster work was popular, and plaster was also used for details and decoration, and as an internal finish.

NEAR LETTERFRACK,
Co. Galway

From this viewpoint little distinguishes this cottage in north Connemara from the surrounding landscape except the smoke rising from its chimney. The building seems an organic structure, made of materials immediately to hand. Rushes and rocks in the foreground and mountainous peaty soil with poor drainage in the background bear witness to the long struggle to eke a living from the unproductive land in this part of the country. Many of the inhabitants were driven to emigration, exchanging this wild beauty for little back-to-back houses in English industrial cities.

Before the nineteenth century bricks were rarely used, except for the larger squares and terraces in Dublin (where they give the city its warm, mellow atmosphere), Limerick and other cities. At first they were imported as ballast in ships returning empty from English ports after unloading agricultural produce for export, but by the mid-nineteenth century they were being manufactured throughout the country. As the century progressed new manufacturing methods meant that bricks were more readily available, including decorative and moulded varieties. They were used for whole terraces of cottages in towns, Dundalk being a good example, and along the canals in Dublin, as well as in the industrial towns of Ulster. They were also used to good effect as window and door surrounds, for eaves details and on chimneys.

Timber was used for fittings and furniture as well as construction; nineteenth-century cottages were given panelled or sheeted wainscoting and fine doors and furniture in mahogany, pitch, pine and deal. Some door designs were borrowed from the formal, classical style, with attractive fan-lights over. The traditional sheeted, ledged and braced doors continued to be made (the wider the sheeting the older the doors). Half-doors were used on smaller farms and cottages. Windows were always of timber until the introduction of iron in the twentieth century. Older windows have two sliding sashes, each with six or eight panes; later sashes had only two panes and recently each sash has but one. More recently some cottage owners have unfortunately allowed themselves to be persuaded to replace original timber sashes with wholly inappropriate aluminium substitutes.

Floors were often simply of beaten earth; though in the kitchen they were sometimes flagged, particularly around the hearth. Bedrooms were often boarded with timber planks, sometimes chosen from the excellent imported timbers that became available in the nineteenth century. Cobbles were also used and often laid in beautiful and elaborate patterns. The designs were formed by laying small rounded stones on edge, and they decorated kitchens, lobbies and the pavement at the entrance to the cottages.

NEAR DOOLIN,
Co. Clare

The coast of Clare is washed by the Atlantic Ocean – not always as calm as it appears here. The cottages along the coast face inland for protection against fierce rain-laden winds. This little group of cottage, outbuilding and boundary wall huddles together for shelter. The house is typical of the gabled types to be seen in Co. Clare, with roofs of thick local slates and dry-dashed walls. The outbuildings and boundary wall are simply and carefully whitewashed.

NEAR LETTERFRACK,
Co. Galway

Up to the beginning of the nineteenth century this area of Connemara, around Clifden, was devoid of roads, living as Robert Kane explains in The Industrial Resources of Ireland *(1845) 'in such a state of seclusion that it contributed no revenue whatsoever to the State and up to 1822 scarcely a stone of oats could be got'. Subsequently, a programme of road building was started, supervised by the engineer Alexander Nimmo. As roads advanced, cottages and farmhouses sprung up beside them and by 1836 Clifden had become an export town, sending out 500 tonnes of oats and returning £7,000 annually to the revenue. This rocky scene with its isolated cottage, now abandoned, gives an inkling of the isolation in which the inhabitants of extensive parts of this western county once lived.*

NEAR COSTELLOE,
Co. Galway

The kitchen window of this simple thatched cottage peeps out between boulder and outbuilding. The roof shows old and more recent thatch, the older being darker in colour. The outbuilding, built separate from the house, is of dry-built, neatly executed stonework, as is the boundary wall, which skirts round the large boulder in the foreground. This area of Connemara, south of the Galway-to-Clifden road, has a beautiful landscape of vast stretches of boggy moorland dotted with many lakelets. The stone in this part of the country is mainly granite, while to the east of Lough Corrib limestone is prevalent. Connemara is also famous for its marbles, largely of greenish colour, which are used for decorative and ornamental work.

INISHMORE,
Co. Galway

Inishmore is the most distant of the Aran Islands from the mainland. This aerial view shows the typical field patterns and dry-built limestone boundary walls of the islands with outbuildings enclosed within the fields. The limestone surface of the island is also discernible, and the islanders had to develop the fields for cultivation of grass, oats and potatoes by building up layers of seaweed and sand over the surface.

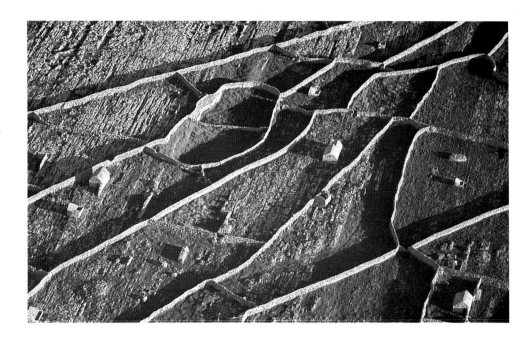

INISHEER,
Co. Galway

This informal group of houses on Inisheer in the Aran Islands, surrounded by tiny enclosed fields with dry-stone walls, is typical of traditional settlement patterns along the western seaboard. The houses, all facing in the same direction, are uniformly of the vernacular, linear, one-room-deep variety, with gabled roofs. All are single-storey, with chimneys on the ridge of the roofs, some of which retain the traditional thatch (rye grass on the Aran Islands), though many are now slated.

INISHEER,
Co. Galway

Inisheer is the closest of the Aran
Islands to the mainland. From it
can be seen north Clare, with its
scatter of houses and cottages old
and new. This maze of very tiny
fields is enclosed by the dry-built
limestone walls which give Aran its
unique character. Lines and layers
of grey textured colour, into which
stone outbuildings merge so they
are barely detectable surround
pools of green. The walls are built
without gates, so the farmer must
break an opening to allow his cattle
in or out and rebuild the wall
afterwards. This requires impressive
skills, passed down from one
generation to the next since the
distant past. The islands have been
inhabited since at least the Bronze
Age, when their ring forts were
built.

INISHEER,
Co. Galway

This unusually large Aran house of
pleasing proportions, slated and
smooth-plastered, was built in
1910–12. Curraghs, the
traditional boats of the west of
Ireland, lie upturned on its sandy
forecourt beside the harbour. The
tradition of boat building is an
ancient and skilled one, and there
are many types of curraghs to suit
different situations. Formerly west
coast curraghs were made from a
framework of hazel rods with a
covering of animal skins, nowadays
they are built of laths covered with
canvas or calico and tarred.

ROCKSTOWN HARBOUR,
Co. Donegal

Under the protection of its rocky outcrop, this Inishowen cottage faces away from the sea, the spray-laden winds blowing against its back. Despite the constant threat of the sea, it stands here as it has done for generations, solid and dignified. Its owners have always known how to combat the remorseless winds. Thatch is tied down with a fine network of criss-cross ropes held by pegs under the eaves; walls were traditionally limewashed, allowing moisture to evaporate away; and thick walls and small windows ensure warmth within.

DUNMANUS BAY,
Co. Cork

This dramatic and rugged headland looks west over Dunmanus Bay towards Sheep's Head. Houses are built as close to the coastline as the cultivation of land will allow. The green fields contrast with the brown, unyielding, rocky ground of this exposed location, and houses face away from the Atlantic winds. Served by a narrow winding road, homes appear remote and isolated, but their inhabitants have always been gregarious, enjoying each other's company when time would allow.

GREAT BLASKET,
Co. Kerry

At the most westerly point in Europe, the Blasket Islands lie off the Dingle Peninsula 'floating in the Atlantic like a school of basking whales' according to Joan and Rae Stagles in The Blasket Islands. *The village on Great Blasket was built into the hillside facing south, with houses in the traditional linear manner: single-storey with thatched roofs of reeds, two rooms — kitchen and bedroom — and a loft over each end, which provided extra sleeping space or storage. Windows were small and rarely on rear walls, and there was usually but one door. The hearth was in the gable tucked into the hillside, and often the slope was so steep that the chimney barely rose above the ground. The Congested Districts Board added to the housing stock in the late nineteenth century. Great Blasket was abandoned in 1953 but the island still attracts visitors, and refurbished houses can accommodate a summer population.*

NEAR CASTLETOWN BEARHAVEN,
Co. Cork

The road, small and narrow, winds, twists and turns its way along the base of hills on its way to Castletown Bearhaven, probably following the route of an ancient track. Fields here are small and bounded by low hedges with hedgerow trees. They are used for pasture on which to graze cattle and to grow a measure of hay, though the rushes indicate poor drainage. The slate-roofed house and red corrugated roofed outbuilding merge quietly into the landscape.

OLD CONNA ESTATE,
Co. Dublin

This impressive snow-clad farmyard, built as a courtyard, has an attractive castellated entrance gate. A range of two-storey outbuildings with characteristic arched doorways serve a variety of uses, including a granary at the end with steps leading up to the entrance. A variety of roof shapes — gabled, half-hipped and conical — add a picturesque note to the buildings which otherwise are of simple expression. Roofs are uniformly slated, and dark painted doors and windows provide a pleasing counterpoint to the white walls.

NEAR OWNING,
Co. Kilkenny

Traditional farm complexes such as this one are among the most pleasing features of the Irish countryside. Usually constructed around a courtyard, each building had a specific use — cow byre, stable, dairy, piggery, henhouse and various storehouses. Here the house looks directly onto the farmyard, which has a unified appearance gained from stone walls, pitched slated roofs and the wonderful use of red paint on all the doors. Its comfortable enclosed atmosphere is greatly enhanced by the mature trees surrounding it.

NEAR LOUGH INAGH,
Co. Galway

The thatching on this little stone outbuilding in the Maumturk Mountains is of the most basic kind. The building has stepped stone gables and would have been put up reasonably quickly. The roof is of marram grass, laid in overlapping layers from eaves to ridges, with a slightly rounded ridge and a number of ropes criss-crossing the thatch horizontally to tie it down. These are taken around the gable stones and fixed to the wall. There are also vertical ropes which are taken over a timber lath at the eaves, to prevent the ropes cutting the thatch, before being fixed to the wall below.

NEAR CLADDAGHDUFF,
Co. Galway

Stones, though uncoursed and irregularly shaped, seem to have been knitted together to form the walls of this linear cottage. The door leads directly into the kitchen from where the chimney barely emerges above the roof ridge. Window openings are tiny, the central one lighting the kitchen and main living space. Gables are stepped, and the ropes which tie down the simply thatched roof are carried across the steps and fixed to the gable, as well as being weighted down by numerous stones across the eaves. Unadorned by flowers or shrubs, the house sits surrounded simply by grass.

LENAN HEAD,
Co. Donegal

Here the dwelling and outbuilding are in one continuous line enclosed by the same walls and covered by the same unbroken roof of thatch. The roof has been recently rethatched and its criss-cross of ropes are fixed regularly over it, attached to pegs just below the eaves. The timber structure of the roof is designed to have a rounded ridge and traditionally such roofs would have had a layer of sods under the thatch, all in order to combat the inevitable gale-force winds. The doorway in the shallow projecting porch leads into the kitchen from where the chimney rises on the right-hand gable. Two other chimneys appear just above the ridge and are barely discernible. The stone pathway leading to the door combines neatly with the grassy forecourt, scarcely disrupting the integrity of the surface.

NEAR BUNRATTY,
Co. Limerick

Here reeds, a popular thatching material in the Munster area where they grow in lakes and rivers, are being harvested, tied in bundles and transported by boat for thatching. Good quality reeds are a desirable material, for a roof carefully covered with them can be expected to give a good life. Local variations in the materials used for thatching are generally dictated by what is most easily available. In the midland counties and Co. Louth wheat straw is used, together with rye and oat, while in mountainous coastal areas of the north-west and west, rushes and tough marram grasses are more common. Flax, which lasts well as a roofing material, is used in some northern counties: Derry, Donegal, Fermanagh and sometimes in Armagh, Antrim, Tyrone and Monaghan.

MAAM CROSS,
Co. Galway

In the past scallops could be bought in bundles of hundreds or thousands at the fairs which were held regularly in country towns. They were of varying materials depending on local preference: willow, bog deal, briar, laurel, hazel or even wire. Scallops were used both in straight lengths and bent into staples. Straight lengths were fixed across the bundles of straw and pinned down to each side, while bent ones were used on the under roof. Both types can be seen here. The tools were a mallet to hammer home the scallops; a knife to trim the thatch; a rake to smooth it and remove loose pieces; and clippers to trim the roof at the eaves. Various improvised tools were also used, such as a broken pitchfork to hold straws in place while working, and sometimes sheep shears to trim the eaves. Sadly, thatching as a roofing method is fast disappearing, and with it the craft.

NEAR NEWPORT,
Co. Tipperary

Here strips of old thatch are being removed and replaced with new straw. The method here is scallop thatching: the straw is fixed to the under-roof of sods in bundles, with cut side down and ear end uppermost, using scallops. Work is carried out from eaves to ridge and the scallops are covered over by the next bundle of straw, so that when the roof is complete all the scallops are disguised except those at the ridge, where they are used to fix the straw that is bent over the top for added strength. The thatcher often took this opportunity to make a decorative band at the ridge — here the design is of lozenge shapes — and sometimes added a matching row at the eaves. The curved gable on this house is an interesting feature: houses of ancient times had similar curved gables, and indeed were often completely circular.

ROSSCARBERY,
Co. Cork

*This house is built adjacent to
Benduff slate quarry near
Rosscarbery. Slates from Cork are
coarse and sometimes unequal in
texture. This house is very simple, of
one and a half storeys with a roof of
local slates and wall and pier
capping of similar material.
During the nineteenth century and
earlier a large number of slate
quarries were in operation in
Ireland. Slates of grey and green-
grey predominated, but those from
Valencia Island in Co. Kerry were
of fine texture and purplish colour
and closer in appearance to the
Welsh Blue Bangors which were
used extensively throughout the
island. Today, quarried slates,
reused or imported, are making a
comeback, being used for
restoration and conservation work
as well as in new buildings. There
are even plans to reopen the quarry
at Portroe, Co. Tipperary.*

ROSSCARBERY,
Co. Cork

*This substantial two-storey house is
also located beside Benduff slate
quarry. With its slate-hung walls
and chimney stacks and slated roof
it appears to be part of the ground
on which it stands. Slate-hanging
is a tradition of southern counties,
where its textured appearance is
distinctive and characteristic,
though it is to be seen occasionally
in other counties. The slates are
fixed onto the walls in overlapping
courses and bedded in lime mortar.
Since slate is an impermeable
material, it gives excellent
protection from wet weather. But
the slate was extracted at a high
cost: there is a monument at
Benduff to eight men who lost their
lives in a quarry accident in 1898
and to individuals lost similarly in
other years. The quarry closed in
the 1940s.*

INISHOWEN,
Co. Donegal

The stable was an important building in the farm complex, as this sturdily built example from Co. Donegal indicates. It is dry-built of roughly coursed rubble of greenish-grey, local slate-like stones of varying sizes, one of which acts as a slim lintel over the door. Dry-building was the most common method of stone building in this area; generally, any mortar that was used was pushed into the joints at a later stage, as here. The slates of the roof, from the local quarry, are of a different texture and colour.

MUNTERMELLAN,
Co. Donegal

This is the rear view of a linear-type Donegal farmhouse. The dwelling has steeply pitched slated roofs with two little windows lighting one of its rooms. The long outbuilding is contained under a continuous roof of thatch and appears to grow out of the ground on which it stands. Trees shelter the house to the right, and green fields, bounded by loosely built dry-stone walls, surround it. This area of Donegal, though beautiful, has much peaty unproductive land which makes living conditions harsh.

LISCANNOR,
Co. Clare

Slate is commonly used on roofs throughout Co. Clare, where good slate was available from local quarries at Liscannor and Killaloe. The slates on this roof are of a greyish colour and are thick as stone tiles: such slates require strong roof structures with timbers of generous dimensions to support them. Very often, as here, they are fixed with pointing between the laps. Sturdy and of an interesting texture, these local slates impart an attractive and unique character to the entire county.

INAGH VALLEY,
Co. Galway

Corrugated iron was used as a roofing material from the end of the nineteenth century when it became available in long lengths. Being light and relatively easy to handle, it provided a useful substitute for thatch. It has had its share of criticism but when painted regularly, particularly in traditional red, it can be attractive as this house in Inagh Valley, Connemara, demonstrates.

NEAR KILCULLEN,
Co. Kildare

Corrugated iron in sheet form was generally used as a roofing material on cottages and outbuildings and for the roofing and cladding of Dutch barns. Sometimes it was used for entire buildings such as small factories, parish halls, creameries and even cottages. This corrugated iron cottage near Kilcullen would have been speedily erected. Freshly painted in carefully chosen colours, it shows how attractive this light and relatively inexpensive material can be.

STREAMSTOWN BAY,
Co. Galway

The roof of this house is covered with grey concrete tiles. Tiles were rarely used as a roofing material until relatively recent times. In the late nineteenth century they were manufactured from clay and concrete, and both home-produced and imported varieties were used as a substitute for more costly slates. Rarely used on public buildings, they became popular as a domestic roofing material during the period 1920–40, particularly in local authority housing. Concrete tiles, available in a range of colours, are still used as a roofing material today. This house has added details in the form of painted quoins at its corners and around its door and window openings. The concrete boundary wall has a number of piers decorated with popular concrete balls. The hay has been saved and formed into haycocks, and a large store of turf has been cut and piled up in readiness for the winter.

NEAR ENFIELD,
Co. Meath

In the midland areas where soil was generally good and plentiful, mud was used for the construction of walls in vernacular houses. It was also a warm material, having a good insulating value. The walls were built in layers, each layer being topped with straw and allowed to dry before the next layer was added. A few stone courses at the base, together with wide overhanging eaves at the top, helped to prevent the mud from deteriorating. For extra stability, walls were battered, being wider at the bottom than at the top. Openings for windows were sometimes cut out after the walls were built. The base of this outbuilding, near Enfield, is constructed of stone courses, with the remainder of mud. The hipped roof was originally of thatch, which has been replaced with corrugated iron.

STREAMSTOWN BAY,
Co. Galway

In the north-west and west of the country, cottages and outbuildings were built with gables. Local stone was used, and it is the size and type of stones used which gives the buildings their individual character, from the large granite boulders built into the base of some cottages and the colourful sandstones in parts of Donegal to the blue-grey limestones of much of the west. The gable of this building is carefully constructed of limestone and granite, using a combination of flat and rounded stones of smallish sizes, laid roughly in courses.

CLADDAGHDUFF,
Co. Galway

This little old thatched house, which must have experienced days of lively comings and goings, is now abandoned. Lime render is falling off the walls, revealing the stone of its structure. On the roof can be seen the criss-cross of ropes once fixed to tie down the thatch to pegs below the eaves, where holes can now be seen. On top of the wall is the regular line of coping stones which would once have been concealed by the overhang of thatch. The timber of the windows and door, without maintenance and painting, begins to rot – first the sills of the windows and the bottom of the door where moisture gathers. Everything is green and white – green plants, green moss, white flower heads, white spots of render. The rust-coloured door, too, will soon be green and white.

BUSHY PARK,
GALWAY CITY,
Co. Galway

This typical gabled cottage of the western counties is of delightfully simple and soft appearance: its lime render over random rubble stonework gives a pleasing undulating effect. Lime plaster was made by burning limestone in kilns to a high temperature to make quick lime. This was then slaked with water and left to mature, when it was used with sand to make a lime plaster. Sometimes other materials were added, such as ox blood and animal hair to strengthen the mix. The plaster was then used to render the walls of the building, applied in a number of layers – two, sometimes three. The walls were then limewashed. This simple method of rendering stone walls was superior and gave better protection to the old walls than modern methods, which use strong Portland cement mixes.

NEAR BORRIS,
Co. Carlow

In Co. Carlow there are good deposits of granite, which is used throughout the county. Stones for building were often hand-cut by the mason in the field where a cottage was being erected. This single-storey cottage near Borris is built of dressed stones of good size, laid in rough courses in an almost random fashion. The chimney stacks are also of stone and the original pointing is still intact. The cottage is from the latter half of the nineteenth century and has a beautiful elliptical arched door opening which, together with the windows, is surrounded with brickwork, painted red. The entrance is lent added importance by its little gabled roof with scalloped barge-boarding.

GLEN OF IMAAL,
Co. Wicklow

Wicklow is a county associated with granite; local quarries supplied a good deal of stone used in Dublin buildings. Granite is the strongest of stones: two of its three components, quartz and felspar, are almost indestructible, and mica, the third, is resistant to chemical attack. It is difficult to carve and so is little used for decorative work. This cottage, built by the county council in 1901, demonstrates the sturdy simplicity of the material. The stones have been mason-dressed and those used for lintels are of generous proportions. With its gabled porch, granite gate piers and attractive gate, the cottage is an example of the high standards achieved in public housing.

SHILLELAGH,
Co. Wicklow

When stone is of good quality the traditional builder decides to leave it exposed, for it can withstand driving rain. The joints are filled with good lime-based mortar when this is available, and any damp which may enter them will not be trapped but evaporate away again. Much of the stone in Co. Wicklow is granite, but parts are of slate. Shillelagh lies in a slate district. The colour of the stone varies: in this terrace it is a mellow brownish ochre, with grey granite for window surrounds. The proportions of the windows are pleasing and in keeping with the hierarchy of spaces, with the ground floor living room window larger than the bedroom windows on the upper floor.

CASTLETOWNSHEND,
Co. Cork

Sandstone from local quarries is common to many buildings in west Cork. The stone, which has varied characteristics and can be used accordingly to give different effects, was quarried at Sherkin Island and near Baltimore along the coast. Here narrow, horizontal slate-like stones are laid randomly in the lime mortar to give an informal 'knitted' texture. This type of stonework gives its character to Castletownshend.

BLOODY FORELAND,
Co. Donegal

Throughout Donegal, sparkling white cottages and farmhouses dot the landscape. The custom is to whitewash houses annually, even in the most remote places. Traditional limewash had a dual function: it had cleansing and sterilizing properties and it also enhanced the cottages themselves as well as the landscapes in which they are set. This cottage has just been given its annual coat of whitewash. The boundary wall has also been included, together with the stones set along the base of the house and edging of the path leading to the door.

SIXMILEBRIDGE,
Co. Clare

A leisurely approach to touching up the paintwork. A traditional brown colour, which goes well with the background of cream wash, has been chosen for window sills and reveals, doorway and step. The ground-floor window sill serves as a seat for a weary passer-by.

NEAR FANORE,
Co. Clare

Red and white colour schemes are quite common in traditional Irish buildings: red on doors, gutters, downpipes and other details, and white on the walls. Here a strong red colour, chosen for the cottage, has been highlighted by the setting sun, but the result, striking and bold, is pleasing, blending as it does with the red and the white on the outbuildings and the white boundary wall. The house is typical of Clare houses: linear, single-storey and gabled, with dark, pitched roof and projecting porch. It sits starkly in the landscape without tree or shrub to soften its edges, surrounded only by a carpet of green grass. Windows have been modernized, while, fortunately, the original window openings have been retained.

NEAR ASKEATON,
Co. Limerick

This simple stone-built house is washed in a soft yellow ochre. Formerly, limewash would have been prepared either from quicklime or the hydrated form, and pigment added to achieve the colour. Applied each year, it built up a silky coating. Nowadays it has been largely replaced by proprietary paints, which are easier to use. This is a pity, since limewash was more compatible with its stone background, to which it also gave protection. The roof of this cottage is of corrugated iron and the attached outbuilding, which may be earlier, has slates. Pet birds are kept in the cages hanging on the wall.

SCHULL,
Co. Cork

Colour has the ability to play tricks on the eye: a diminutive building can be lent importance and perhaps even made to appear larger by the use of strong colour. Here this little cottage, hemmed in by two taller neighbours, could be lost and insignificant, but instead it chooses a coat of rich deep dark blue, for which the white woodwork of windows and doors is the perfect foil. Now it commands attention.

UNION HALL,
Co. Cork

Paint is a versatile material and with little effort and financial outlay a building can be given a new personality simply by changing its colour scheme. There is a long tradition in the use of colour in buildings throughout Ireland, but nowhere more so than in the towns of west Cork. Here buildings are painted annually in preparation for festivals and for summer. Streets, such as this one at Union Hall, are painted in a blend of colours, the successful matching and contrasting of which is often achieved more by instinct than by intention.

NEAR MIZEN HEAD,
Co. Cork

The west Cork area is well known for its adventurous use of colour. This two-storey house is four bays wide with an attached two-storey outbuilding: the blue and creamy yellow colour scheme is continued throughout, but the dwelling part is given emphasis with large blue panels.

NEAR ANTRIM TOWN
Co. Antrim

Basalt, a black stone quarried on the Antrim plateau, was commonly used for houses throughout the county in both coursed rubble work and dressed stone. This fine two-storey farmhouse is built of coursed basalt stone with door and window surrounds. The stonework has been given a coat of black paint and the pointing picked out in white, with window surrounds in strong red. The windows have been modernized but the original openings have fortunately been retained. Basalt is also used in Co. Derry and Co. Down.

CASTLECOMER,
Co. Kilkenny

Brick was imported as ballast on ships returning from England and used in numerous eighteenth-century city buildings. It was also used in some early country houses for decoration, as at Beaulieu, Drogheda, Co. Louth. It was rarely used in cottage building before the mid-nineteenth century, however. By then there were numerous brickworks throughout the country, and brick was used for chimneys and fireplaces. Towards the end of the century brick manufacturing had become an industrial process: the bricks were now uniform in size and colour and, while less interesting in texture than older handmade ones, were available in a range of decorative and moulded forms. This terrace of red-brick cottages in Castlecomer dates from the end of the nineteenth century and incorporates decorative bricks in chimneys and hood moulds over windows.

CASTLETOWNSHEND,
Co. Cork

Brick has frequently been used for chimney stacks, particularly from the nineteenth century. In cottages, it is generally used in a simple manner; but often, too, the chimneys were designed as features, with moulded bricks, string courses, fancy brickwork and so forth. Many of the romantic estate village cottages give great importance to their chimney stacks, both in height and size. To be effective, chimney stacks should stand at least three feet higher than the roof ridge. These chimney stacks on a house in Castletownshend easily exceed this. The bricks are built in courses at staggered angles to give an unusual, honeycomb look.

BALLYCONNEELY,
Co. Galway

This cottage window peeps out from under the eaves of a thatched roof tied down with ropes. Charmingly framed with lace curtains, the blue-painted window is of casement type and is a relatively recent replacement for the earlier up-and-down sliding sashes. The original opening size has fortunately been retained, maintaining the pleasing proportions of the cottage. The opening is simple and without sill, providing a comfortable spot for the cat.

Donegal Window

The up-and-down sliding sash window was common to traditional cottages from the early nineteenth century. Until then the houses of the poor were frequently windowless, or if windows existed they were without glass. This window has small Georgian panes, a double row of three wide in the bottom sash and a single row in the top sash, which has ears to the underside to give strength. The design derives from the formal architecture of the eighteenth century, which had a lasting influence on designs in town and country. Later in the nineteenth century the small panes were replaced by one in each sash. Here the window is made of timber and painted, and a splash of colour is added in the red of the sill, the reveal and the lath fixed under the ropes tying down the thatch.

Nineteenth- and Twentieth-Century Developments

ADARE,
Co. Limerick

This terrace of thatched estate cottages is an unusual example of the English picturesque style. The village was built outside the gates of Adare Manor, the house of the Earls of Dunraven, at the beginning of the nineteenth century, replacing a motley collection of about twenty-four thatched cottages. The present village was probably inspired by popular pattern books such as P F Robinson's Rural Architecture (1823), influenced by Uvedale Price's essay on the picturesque. By 1848 the village had grown to one thousand inhabitants and the setting had matured well; according to a contemporary observer, the cottages, which were 'partly interspersed with fine old trees and flower gardens, have a most picturesque appearance' and were neat and clean.

The nineteenth century was to see many improvements in the lives of those who dwelt in cottages and houses in both town and country. The Act of Union of 1800 ended the Irish Parliament, with the result that many members of Parliament, all of the landowning classes, decamped to London, from where the country was to be governed for the following 120 years. The early decades of the nineteenth century saw the Irish population rising to unprecedented numbers (8.5 million in 1845), causing terrible overcrowding. The devastating years of famine that followed, and the ensuing years of emigration reduced this figure by half by the 1920s. In the latter half of the century new legislation brought about the redistribution of land to individual farms and ownerships, and the state acted to alleviate substandard housing conditions caused by overcrowding in towns and cities.

At the beginning of the nineteenth century landlords were continuing to improve their estates, and now turned their attention to their estate workers. New purpose-built estate villages sprang up to replace the groups of primitive cabins that had housed the workers hitherto. Such improvements were not wholly altruistic, since the landlords were well aware that such villages conveyed an agreeable impression of the estate owner's taste and nobility of character to arriving visitors. Nevertheless, they considerably improved the living standards of those few lucky enough to be housed in them, who must indeed have been the envy of those less fortunate.

Designs were based on the pattern books then commonly available, and many are in an English picturesque Tudor style, with steeply pitched roofs, tall chimney stacks, dormer windows, gabled porches, and decorative barge boarding, though some landlords preferred classical styles.

The accommodation in estate villages might include examples of single-storey, one-and-half-storey and two-storey cottages, detached, in pairs or terraced. Inside there was usually a kitchen, a parlour and one or two bedrooms, and outside perhaps half an acre of land to be cultivated by the occupiers for their own use. The cottages were sturdily built, many of excellent quality stone, with dressed stones for sills, quoins, plinths, door and window surrounds and mouldings. City and town estates also provided cottages in pairs or terraces for their employees.

Within the walls of the country estates other small houses were built for agents and other employees. Shooting and fishing lodges provided hospitality for hunting parties; shell cottages might serve the same purpose or be purely ornamental; and gate lodges oversaw arrivals and departures, the importance of their role often reflected in their architectural expression rather than in their provision of accommodation. Gentlemen's residences were built in the cottage orné style, a romantic conflation of grandiose scale and vernacular style. Two such cottages are open to the public: Swiss Cottage in Cahir Park, Co. Tipperary, and Derrymore House in Camlough, Co. Armagh.

Despite the fact that most of the country experienced little or no industrial revolution, industry played a modest part in the building boom. Domestic linen weaving, an important industry in the north-east from the eighteenth century, occupied large numbers of weavers, whose cottages typically incorporated a shop or shed with an outshot (alcove) similar to a bed outshot. Cotton mills were converted to the linen industry and new flax mills were built. Silcock's Mill, also called Marybrook Mill, near Ballinahinch in Co. Down, is a water-powered flax scutching and corn mill that has been restored to fully operational condition by its owners.

Larger milling concerns built industrial villages of terraced cottages for their workers. Sion Mills in Co. Tyrone, with mill and cottages fronted by attractive greens, is one such, developed from 1835 by the Hederman family, and now a conservation area. Outside the north-east, attempts at industrialization were unsuccessful, with the exception of Portlaw in Co. Waterford, where the Quaker Malcolmson family developed cotton spinning mills in 1825. To accommodate the workforce they built a model industrial village designed in a semi-circle, with streets of simple terraced cottages radiating from the central market square.

Developments in transport and communications brought about major advancements. An ambitious programme of canal building was embarked on as early as 1729. The first scheme, the Newry Navigation Scheme, an 18-mile stretch from Newry to Lough Neagh, was begun and completed between 1731 and 1742, the first such undertaking in the British Isles. By the 1760s Newry was linked to the sea by a ship canal, also the first such in the British Isles. Other major schemes followed, with the result that good building materials could now be much more readily transported throughout the country.

Canal locks were operated manually by lock-keepers who lived with their families in cottages specially built for them beside the locks. The prototype was probably provided by Thomas Omer, an engineer employed on the canal navigation schemes. The cottages were quite charming, both in their architecture and in their waterside position.

The canals were soon to be superseded by the railways, and fell into disuse and dereliction, from which some stretches are happily now being rescued. The railways probably made the single greatest contribution to easier communications. The first stretch to be built, to the designs of Charles Vignoles, was from Dublin to Kingstown, now Dun Laoghaire, in 1834. Terraces of cottages quickly sprang up along the coasts, now easily reached from the city, and as the line was extended, ever more building took place. Seaside towns, which previously had provided lodges only for the better-off, were now accessible to everyone, and the ever-growing numbers of visitors had to be accommodated. Many seaside cottages, dating from the 1840s, were built in regency and classical styles and sometimes with extremely high quality stucco work.

The railway companies also provided accommodation for their workers. Such cottages, probably designed by engineers as part of general railway work, were terraced in streets and around squares and can still be seen at Great Western Square, Phibsboro, Dublin, where two-storey terraced cottages of red brick are built around a green enclosed by railings. Where a railway line crossed a road a third category of cottage was built to accommodate the level crossing operator. Also in Dublin, the United Dublin Tramway Company built terraces of simple, single-storey cottages for its workers at Rathgar, Inchicore, Clontarf and Donnybrook, as well as at Blackrock in Co. Dublin.

New suburbs were growing meanwhile on the outskirts of towns and cities to accommodate the growing middle classes. But while the middle classes were moving to the suburbs, the city centres were crammed with the poorer, labouring classes living in dreadful conditions. From the 1870s the government set about improving the standards of dwellings of artisans and labourers. The Dublin Artisan Dwelling Company, founded in 1876, was responsible for providing new cottages at reasonable rents to artisans.

Local authorities were also instrumental in improving housing standards in towns and cities. Waterford Corporation claims to have been the first to meet the challenge with the provision of new cottages at Green's Lane, now Green's Street, in 1878–9. Private charitable institutions, for example the Iveagh Trust in Dublin city, contributed to the housing stock as well, and during the last decades of the century even the private sector was engaged in building cottages at low rents for the working classes.

In the countryside, cottage dwellers too benefited from certain social improvements, following the famine years. The numbers of mud cabins declined, the land was generally improved and drained and because of the declining population, farm holdings could be enlarged. There was still the problem of land ownership, however, and areas of cultivated land remained in the hands of a very small minority. The Land Commission, established in 1887, was given powers to purchase and redistribute land by giving loans to tenant farmers, and by 1896 80,000 holdings had been purchased in this way.

The Land Commission, the newly created County Councils and the Rural District Councils all built cottages in order to improve the living standards of poor rural workers, farm labourers, county council workers and crafts people. This early public housing was single-storey or one-and-a-half storeys high, and was in a simple picturesque style, reminiscent of estate cottages. The cottages were either rendered in lime plaster or built of stone, their roofs steeply pitched and slated, and some had porches, although in many the front door opened straight into the kitchen.

Chimney stacks and window and door surrounds were often of brick; windows were timber and had up-and-down sliding sashes. The accommodation consisted of a kitchen and two bedrooms or one bedroom and a parlour, and where there was an upper floor it was reached by stairs from the kitchen. Each cottage had a small outbuilding or piggery, a privy and an acre of ground attached.

In 1891 the Congested Districts Board was set up to tackle the worst of the problems in the west of Ireland, where large numbers of people were living at barely subsistence level. It upgraded the infrastructure, improved roads, developed light railways, encouraged fishing and rural industries and relocated large numbers of people to ease overcrowding. To improve housing standards, it built cottages which were sturdy and of simple plan, with an acre of ground attached. The Board later extended its work to other parts of Ireland.

In 1914 electricity was introduced into city cottages and, influenced by the 'Garden City Movement', new cottage schemes were planned with gardens. In the 1920s and 1930s new materials became available for use in public housing: roof tiles replaced slates; cement render replaced lime plaster; steel window frames replaced timber. In the 1950s entrance porches were added and casement windows replaced up-and-down sliding sashes.

In 1946, Bórd na Moṅa, the state-sponsored Irish Turf Board was established to develop large areas of bogland to provide peat for domestic and industrial use. From its inception it employed large numbers of workers, and in eight locations throughout the midlands where bogs were intensively worked, it built villages for some of its employees. Ballivor in Co. Meath is the smallest, consisting of only eight cottages and the largest is Coill Dubh in Kildare, with 156 cottages. The villages were spaciously laid out with curving two-storey terraces and attractive greens, hedges, trees and informal pathways.

In recent years there has been a good deal of cottage building, and public housing schemes (unlike the lamentable and ubiquitous bungalow) have generally been of a high standard with improved accommodation and facilities. Such schemes conceived and built as a single design with uniform and usually pleasing materials, are worthy successors to the modest but practical and charming tradition of Irish cottage building.

BALLYPOREEN,
Co. Tipperary

Nissen huts (named after their inventor, the British mining engineer Peter Nissen), were quick and easy to assemble and were intended to provide shelter for the military. Some have now been put to other uses. This one, anchored here amid shrubs and stately lilies, makes a comfortable home. The pump is probably now ornamental, but before the days of piped water such pumps would have provided water from an underground source for the surrounding area.

ADARE,
Co. Limerick

This charming two-storey cottage in Adare has a rusticated entrance porch and hipped thatch roof. Large and impressive and located in the centre of the village, it was more than likely built for an important employee on the estate. It is interesting that these early estate cottages have kept their thatch roofs, since it would have been easier to replace them with slates. Adare still retains much of its character, and gives a good indication of what an estate village must have been like when first built.

BALLYMASCANLON,
Co. Louth

This window from the Ballymascanlon Estate cottages is in a romantic perpendicular Gothic style typical of the designs used for estate cottages. The lights are leaded, with the leading picked out in white, and the two main panels are divided by a central mullion.

FENNAGH,
Co. Carlow

The romantic profusion of a traditional cottage garden is the perfect complement to any cottage. Here at Fennagh the gardens add considerably to the charm of this terrace of estate cottages, originally attached to Fennagh House. The cottages, sturdily built of granite, indicate the quality of the contribution made by the estates to the general housing stock.

Pembroke Gardens,
DUBLIN

In 1913 a triangular area of ground behind Pembroke Road in Dublin was developed by a Trust founded by Lady Pembroke to house needy citizens. Twenty-three cottages were built with small front gardens and a shared park to the rear. Situated in a pleasingly secluded location away from noisy traffic routes, the houses are built in pairs, and of red brick, and incorporate a number of interesting features including steeply pitched roofs. Being in the care of a Trust the design integrity of the development has been carefully maintained. The Trust itself continued to operate up to about ten years ago when care of the cottages was taken over by the Pembroke Estate Company.

GLENVEAGH ESTATE,
Co. Donegal

As soon as Glenveagh Castle was erected in 1870 a walled garden was created, together with a gardener's cottage. This reputedly had a flat concrete roof, which would have been most unusual, but was later to be pitched and roofed with corrugated iron before its present four inches of thatch was added in the 1950s. The cottage is occupied by Mr Armour, the estate gardener of many years, now retired, and the garden is in the care of the Office of Public Works and open to the public.

GLENVEAGH ESTATE,
Co. Donegal

This small two-room shooting lodge on the Glenveagh Estate in the Derryveagh Mountains is of linear plan but has classical details in its window design and doors with their semicircular fanlights. The chimney stack is centred on the ridge and the roof is slated. It stands in a clearing overlooking the Owencarrow River and is a recent addition to the estate, built in about 1950 by Henry McIlhenny. Glenveagh Estate was developed by John George Adair in 1857–9, having first reputedly been cleared of 254 tenants. Glenveagh Castle itself was built to designs of Adair's cousin, John Townsend Trench, in 1870–73 and commands a dramatic view over the lake from its promontory site. The estate, which includes Mount Errigal and Slieve Snaght, the two highest peaks in Donegal, as well as the castle and gardens, is now state-owned and open to the public.

CARTON ESTATE,
Co. Kildare

The shell cottage at Carton, formally a thatched cottage called Waterstown, stands on a height in the woods overlooking an oriental-style footbridge over the Ryewater. Shell cottages, decorated with shells collected by their eager creators, enjoyed a vogue during the eighteenth century as rather whimsically rustic settings for entertaining visitors to the great estates. In its heyday, this one saw many visitors entertained to lunch and supper, the most eminent being Queen Victoria, in whose honour a large room was added in 1849. The Victorian era also saw the addition of cast-iron 'tree trunks' to support the overhanging eaves and a pavement with the date 1849 and the royal crest inlaid in pebbles. The shell room has a domed light and is beautifully executed, particularly in the work to the ceiling. Edward Malins and the Knight of Glin suggest that the Carton shell house 'must once have been as gay as the dancing light on the cascading river alongside'.

CARTON ESTATE,
Co. Kildare

Carton is one of the two great estates in Co. Kildare, the other being neighbouring Castletown. The development of each owed much to the Lennox sisters – Louisa at Castletown, and Emily, together with her husband the first duke of Leinster, at Carton. Standing on the River Ryewater, enlarged by a system of dams to create a lake, is the boat house, first built as part of the landscaping of the estate in the eighteenth century (the stone bridge beside it was built to the designs of Thomas Ivory in 1763). Later improvements resulted in the present Tudor Gothic style, with steeply pitched roofs and decorative barge-boarding. The ground-floor arched openings indicate its function as a boat house, while the upper floor was used for entertainment and storing fishing gear. The estate grounds also include an eighteenth-century ornamental dairy and the shell house.

KENMARE ESTATE, KILLARNEY, Co. Kerry

Deenagh Lodge was built in 1834 for Colonel Valentine Browne, at the entrance to Kenmare Estate from Killarney town. It is a tall single-storey cottage in a romantic rustic style, very much in the manner of John Nash and Humphry Repton. The steeply pitched thatched roof curves charmingly over projecting lattice-paned oriel windows supported on brackets. A rustic timber veranda each side is supported on timber tree-trunk posts. The inviting gabled and projecting open porch leads to a round-headed doorway. Very tall chimneys introduce an asymmetrical element to an otherwise balanced façade. Up to 1988, when it was tragically burnt down, this was the last remaining of a number of ornamental cottages on the Kenmare Estate. Happily, the Office of Public Works has undertaken its reconstruction.

DE VESCI ESTATE, ABBEYLEIX, Co. Laois

This cottage, on the De Vesci Estate, is in a typical estate Tudor style, with gabled upper-floor windows, scalloped barge-boarding and leaded windows. The upper rooms are contained within the steeply pitched roof space. The lush green woodland setting adds further to the cottage's considerable charms. The building to the right is a more recent addition, happily in keeping. The estate garden is open to the public.

GARINISH ISLAND,
Co. Kerry

This island in Kenmare Bay – not to be confused with Garinish Island in Bantry Bay, also known as Ilnacullen, which is in state ownership – was developed by the Dunraven family of Adare in Co. Limerick. The 3rd Earl purchased it and built a house on it, and later developments by the 4th Earl completed the landscape's transformation from cattle pasture to the magnificent gardens which cover it today. This house, peeping out over a grey stone wall through the palm trees, was built in about 1865. It is in an attractive estate cottage style, with steeply pitched roofs, gabled entrance doorway and dormer windows. Partly single-storey and partly two storeys, it takes advantage of varying ground levels to add interest to the design.

Swiss Cottage,
CAHIR,
Co. Tipperary

Considered to be one of the most perfect examples of the cottage orné style in these islands, Swiss Cottage was built for Richard Butler, Earl of Glengall, in about 1810. It was designed by the English architect John Nash, who designed a number of other buildings in the Cahir area. Overlooking the River Suir, the cottage is built in a rusticated picturesque style and incorporates many of Nash's favourite features with thatched roof of reeds, wide overhanging eaves, dormer windows and an open verandah, whose roof of cedarwood shingles is supported on oak columns. The building had fallen into disrepair, but has recently been restored and is now a national monument open to the public.

MULLINGAR,
Co. Westmeath

Gate lodges always stood at the entrances to estates, either on the same side of the road as the main house, inside the gates or, as Maurice Craig points out, 'opposite them on the other side of the public road'. It has been suggested, he says, that by this 'the owners wanted to demonstrate to the world at large that they owned land on both sides of the road', though he doubts this himself. True or not, the gate lodge, which often has no more accommodation than a simple cottage, is clearly intended to impress the world at large. Ballynegall House, to which this fine ashlar lodge is attached, was built by James Gibbons in 1808 using stones from the old Castle Reynell. The lodge is in the classical style and has a hipped and slated roof with exposed rafter feet and centrally positioned chimney stack.

BELLINE ESTATE,
PILTOWN,
Co. Kilkenny

Large estates had a number of entrances with gate lodges, usually containing the humblest of accommodation cloaked in an impressive exterior, as is clearly demonstrated by this lodge on the Belline Estate. The temple, a building which would normally serve spiritual needs, is the chosen style and is here given a charming rusticated flavour by using tree trunks to act as columns. Two rows of these tree trunks, which have capitals of rope, support the pediment and create an interesting wood-like atmosphere of light and shade in a natural and informal setting. It is to be hoped that the future of this lodge will be assured while maintaining this charming ambience. Belline House itself dates from the late eighteenth century and is noteworthy for having an unusual detached three-storey circular pavilion on each side.

CASTLEBORO ESTATE, NEAR ENNISCORTHY, Co. Wexford

Castleboro House was built in about 1840, in an outdated Palladian style, to the designs of Daniel Robertson for the first Lord Carew. It is now a ruin, after a fire in 1923. Sadly the gate lodge, too, is in a ruinous state. Designed in classical style in keeping with the main house, its most important façade, Doric-porticoed and pedimented, is almost all that remains. Nature is gradually encroaching on it and taking over. In Vanishing Country Houses of Ireland (1989), the Knight of Glin, David Griffin and Nicholas Robinson urge that 'the house, now a ruin, must be preserved as it is one of the most magnificent ruins in the country'.

POWERSCOURT ESTATE, Co. Wicklow

Powerscourt Estate in Co. Wicklow, with its beautiful gardens overlooking the Great and Little Sugar Loaf Mountains, was developed by Richard Wingfield, Viscount Powerscourt, in the eighteenth century. The house, designed by Richard Cassels and begun in 1731, was tragically destroyed by fire, together with its priceless contents, in 1974. At the entrance to the demesne stands this gate lodge in the picturesque style, with steeply pitched roofs covered with small scallop-shaped slates. While the accommodation is simple, the exterior has been lent importance and character by the application of hood moulds and barge-boarding, and by the tall chimney stack and gable-fronted open porch with Gothic arch. The raised site, requiring six steps up to the entrance, gives it added presence.

RAVENSDALE ESTATE,
Co. Kildare

Gate lodges are predominantly of one or one-and-a-half storeys, more often than not in a romantic Tudor or Classical style. This one at the entrance to the Ravensdale Estate differs from the norm in being a full two storeys high and wavering in style between the vernacular and the classical. Its hipped and slated roof and its height show a classical influence; the proportions of its front façade are simple and pleasing, with large areas of wall and relatively small and few windows. The narrow side elevation faces the road while the front overlooks the demesne entrance. The gates are modest in scale but have good cut-stone ball decorations on the caps of the piers.

GLENVEAGH ESTATE,
Co. Donegal

This gate lodge near Garton, at one of the entrances to Glenveagh Estate, is said to have had a flat concrete roof, together with other cottages on the estate, including the gardener's cottage illustrated on p. 126. This unusual feature was replaced by a pitched corrugated iron roof before 1940 and the present thatch roof was added in the 1950s. The iron roof still remains under four inches of thatch. It is likely that the external decoration was added at the same time. The cottage is L-shaped, with roofs joining in an unusual way, simply executed and very much in keeping with other cottages on the estate.

Clashganny Lock,
NEAR BORRIS,
Co. Carlow

The engineering and building works associated with the canals were an impressive achievement; beautifully cut stone walls, superbly constructed timber lock gates in traditional black and white colour and trim keepers' cottages together make a fine sight. This lock is on a stretch of canal near Borris in Co. Carlow, where short stretches were built around falls on the River Barrow.

DRUMBEG,
Co. Antrim

Drumbeg lock house stands on the Lagan navigation system, constructed between 1756 and 1793. With some six others between Lisburn and Belfast, the cottage was built in about 1760 to the designs of Thomas Ower, whose name is closely associated with the inland navigation systems of the eighteenth century. He also designed Shannon navigation lock houses at Banagher, where his son Daniel worked with him, and at Shannonbridge, and similar houses were built on the Grand Canal, completed in 1835. All have a characteristic appearance, being of two storeys on a square plan with pitched slate roofs and recessed arches positioned centrally on each façade. This cottage is built of random stonework with red sandstone quoins and string courses. The arches and chimneys are of brick. It was badly damaged by fire before being taken over and restored by Hearth, a charitable association involved in building conservation.

INISHEER,
Co. Galway

By their very nature, lighthouses stand in some of the wildest, loneliest spots: comfortable accommodation for the keeper was therefore a necessity. The lighthouse here on Inisheer – the most southern of the Aran Islands – was built together with a keeper's cottage in 1857. Both are of local crystalline limestone, which is extremely durable, and are rendered and painted in the black-and-white colour scheme that is characteristic of many such complexes. The lighthouse was automated in 1978 and the keeper now lives over a mile away.

CROOKHAVEN,
Co. Cork

Most Irish lighthouses, together with ancillary buildings, were built between 1810 and 1860. The complexes were constructed to the designs of the Inspector of Lighthouses, George Halpin and (from 1830) his son, whose standard plans were used up to the 1870s. Walls were of random rubble, finished externally with dressed stone, slate hanging or rendered, and internally with dressed stone or plastered. Here at Crookhaven, the complex was unusually large because dwellings were also provided for the principal keeper and other keepers of the Fastnet Rock lighthouse, which is off-shore. Crookhaven lighthouse, together with other lighthouses, began to be operated on a relief system, and by 1981 its keeper, like keepers of all other manned stations and their families, had moved to live elsewhere, thus ending a long established tradition.

Silcock's Mill,
CROSSGAR,
Co. Down

This beautiful complex comprises a
corn mill and flax scutching mill,
both water-powered, and the
miller's house. The buildings and
the mill mechanisms, redundant for
many decades, have been carefully
restored by their present owners
and are now fully operational. The
Silcocks, who developed the mill in
the eighteenth century, were a
Scottish planter family. In the mid-
nineteenth century they built a new
corn mill together with a scutch
mill, and also a house to replace the
earlier cottage. The mills gave good
employment in their day and a
number of cottages were provided
for workers. The original mill
cottage still stands, now connected
to the house by a new wing added
by its present owners.

MONKSTOWN,
Co. Dublin

After the first stretch of railway was
built from Dublin to Monkstown in
1834, new suburbs grew up beside
it. Here at Seapoint, a narrow strip
of land between the railway line
and the sea was developed for
housing from the 1840s. The area
is approached over a small stone
bridge, which was built in 1836 to
give access to an adjacent Martello
tower and is probably the oldest
railway bridge in these islands.
Built in pairs, the houses are two-
storeys high with flights of steps
leading up to hall doors, and they
seem to snuggle down into their
ground floor garden levels like cosy
cottages. Of granite construction,
they are rendered in high quality
stucco work with moulded details,
and some have plaster-cast lions
and other features. The pathways to
a number of houses have
interesting cobbling, and all have
good cast-iron railings.

Highfield Grove, RATHGAR, DUBLIN

The Dublin United Tramway Company operated an efficient public transport system throughout the city until the end of the 1940s, when it was disbanded and the tram tracks were dismantled. Like other transport companies, the DUTC built homes for its workers and, again, like other such companies, did not give them a great deal of thought at the time of building. It is true to say, however, that these cottages can be most attractive. Highfield Grove is typical of such developments: pleasantly laid out around a landscaped green, the cottages are tucked away from the traffic but at the same time close to all necessary facilities. The mellow brick gives them a soft, warm appearance.

RINGSEND DUBLIN

Ringsend was once a small port on the outskirts of Dublin. Today incorporated into the city, its streets are lined mainly with nineteenth-century buildings, many of which are red-brick cottages. Simple two-storey terraces have been given an air of flamboyance through the decorative treatment of window and door surrounds. Segmental arched windows are a feature, and houses have slate roofs and brick chimneys. The gasometer in the background, for many years a landmark and now redundant, is being dismantled.

NEAR ADARE,
Co. Limerick

County council cottages of the late
nineteenth century differed little
from vernacular styles. This one
has the same simple plan, with just
two rooms, a kitchen and bedroom,
and is entered directly without
porch or hall. The roof is now slated
rather than thatched and the
chimney is of brick. A little
embellishment has been added in
the form of window and door
surrounds and the door has a
rectangular fanlight over it.

NEAR CARNEW,
Co. Wicklow

This country cottage on the road to
Bunclody was built by Wicklow
County Council in 1901. It is one
and a half storeys high with two
rooms each on the ground and
upper floors, and has the usual acre
of ground attached, an outbuilding,
which originally served as a
piggery, and a privy in the yard at
the rear. Today this is used as a
pumphouse for water supply to the
house. The cottage is built of stone,
rendered and painted. The present
owner, Ned Kilbride, who worked as
a gardener all his life, is a son of the
original owner.

Council Cottage
Co. Donegal

This example of public housing was provided by a rural district council (forerunners of county councils) towards the end of the nineteenth century. It is one and a half storeys high, in the picturesque style, with steeply pitched slated roofs, including one over the entrance door. Barge-boarding and windows with small panes add extra interest. The entrance door leads directly into the kitchen, where stairs lead up to the bedroom floor. The house has two rooms up and two rooms down and, influenced by the linear tradition, is but one room deep.

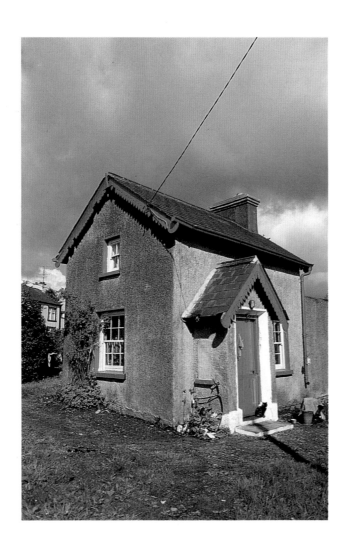

NEAR LOUGH FINN,
Co. Donegal

This small roadside farmhouse, with pitch-roofed porch and paired windows, is reminiscent of turn-of-the-century public buildings. Painted white, it is in keeping with Donegal tradition, and the door and window surrounds painted blue give it an individual stamp. The garage to one side and the little cultivated garden to the other, each bounded by a hedge, create a sense of enclosure. The tractor, commonly in use since the 1960s, has become indispensable to the farmer and very much a feature of the countryside.

RATHDRUM,
Co. Wicklow

This cottage from the 1930s has a slated gabled roof with a pair of chimney stacks and a gabled entrance porch placed centrally in the façade. The timber windows have up-and-down sliding sashes and larger double windows are separated by timber mullions, thus retaining the traditional vertical emphasis of the windows. The walls are rendered in sand and cement, rough-cast and painted.

ASHFORD,
Co. Wicklow

This cottage indicates the extraordinary ingenuity that may be devoted to turning a simple structure into a thing of beauty. The house dates from about the 1930s and has a half-hipped roof of slates with ridge tiles and a chimney at each end. The design is balanced in the classical manner, with a central doorway and paired windows at each side. This single-storey house type, often with bay windows, was built in both town and country by private individuals. It was a forerunner of the modern bungalow, but because of the limited materials used in its construction it is generally much more at ease in its surroundings than its present day counterpart.

NEAR ADARE,
Co. Limerick

That this little window is utterly charming one could hardly deny, yet such windows have rarely, if ever, been used as a reference for the windows of modern houses. In scale and proportion it is perfect; it is practical in our climate; it is interesting internally, allowing in pools of light and giving a constant play of light and shade; and it leaves greater areas of wall free inside the cottage.

Photographer's Notes

My first photograph of a thatched Irish cottage was taken during a holiday on Inishmore, Aran Islands, twenty-five years ago. In retrospect this was in fact the beginning of this book. Regrettably, I let ten years pass before the idea manifested itself. The reality of these beautiful cottages, which were so much part of the island I had come to live in, but which were falling into dereliction and being forgotten, moved me to put on film what was disappearing forever. Never again have I seen mackerel being put onto a thatched roof for drying and preserving as I saw it that fine day on Inishmore.

On many thousand miles of journeys across Ireland in all kinds of weather and seasons, I looked out for original and unspoiled cottages. Leafy lanes and sodden bog roads would tempt me to explore, and I was often rewarded with the discovery of a cottage and scene to be photographed.

Houses are built by people and often take on their friendly character, so I always felt very welcome. Indeed their owners would invariably offer me a cup of tea, which would be accompanied by many stories of the past – a past rich in tradition and reflecting a way of life which was fading away like the cottages themselves.

The natural settings and the landscape which inspired me so much started to change, creating a new awareness of what had been lost. I hope that this book will help to preserve what still remains.

All photographs have been taken with Nikon lenses ranging from 20mm to 300mm. The film used was Ektachrome Professional 135 and Fujichrome Professional RDP 100. Filters were used only to correct colour balance or contrast.

Last, but not least, a sincere 'Thank You' to all the people whose cottages are featured in this book.

Bibliography

Bannon, M.J. (ed.), *The Emergence of Irish Planning 1880–1920* (Turoe Press, Dublin 1985)

Bense-Jones, Mark, *Burke's Guide to Country Houses* (Burke's Peerage Ltd., London 1978)

Blades, Brook S., 'In the Manner of England – Tenant Housing in the Londonderry Plantation', in *Ulster Folk Life*, vol. 27, 1981, Alan Gailey (ed.)

Bord Failte & An Taisce (The National Trust), *Building Sensitively in Ireland's Landscapes* (Bord Failte & An Taisce, Dublin 1985)

Brett, C.E.B., *Hearth* (Northern Ireland Historic Environmental and Architectural Rehabilitation Trust, Belfast 1988)

Brett, C.E.B., *Historic Buildings in the Towns of Monaghan* (U.A.H.S. & An Taisce, Belfast & Dublin 1970)

Butlin, R.A. (ed.), *The Development of the Irish Town* (Croom Helm, London 1977)

Corkery, Daniel, *The Hidden Ireland* (Gill & Macmillan, Dublin 1924, this edn 1967, reprinted 1984)

Craig, Maurice, *The Architecture of Ireland from Earliest Times to 1880* (Batsford, London 1982)

Craig, Maurice, 'Some Smaller Country Houses' in *Country Life*, 8 July 1949, pp.131–2

Craig, Maurice, *Classic Houses of the Middle Size* (The Architectural Press, London 1976)

Craig, Maurice & The Knight of Glin, *Ireland Observed* (Mercier Press, Cork 1970)

Cullen, L.M., *Life in Ireland* (Batsford, London 1968, first paperback edn 1979)

Danaher, Kevin, *Ireland's Vernacular Architecture* (Mercier Press, Cork 1975)

Danaher, Kevin, *The Hearth and Stool and All,* (Mercier Press, Dublin 1985)

Darley, Gillian, *Villages of Vision* (Architectural Press, London 1975)

De Breffny, Brian (ed.), E. Estyn Evans and others, *The Irish World* (Thames & Hudson, London 1977)

De Breffney, Brian and Rosemary Ffolliott, *The Houses of Ireland* (Thames and Hudson, London 1975)

Delaney, V. & R., *The Canals of the South of Ireland* (David & Charles, Newton Abbot 1966)

Department of the Environment (N.I.), *Sion Mills Conservation Area* (N. Ireland D.O.E., Belfast 1977)

Dixon, Hugh, *An Introduction to Ulster Architecture* (U.A.H.S., Belfast 1975)

Dowling, Daniel & Hurley, *Housing in Waterford* (Waterford Corporation, Waterford 1988)

Dunraven, Caroline Quinn Countess of, *Memorials of Adare Manor* (1865)

Evans, E. Estyn, *Irish Heritage* (Dundalgan Press, Dundalk 1942)

Evans, E. Estyn & Brian S. Turner, *Ireland's Eye* (Blackstaff Press, Belfast 1977)

Gailey, Alan, *Rural Houses of the North of Ireland* (John Donald Ltd., Edinburgh 1984)

Gailey, Alan, & Kenneth Darwin, *Wilson House* (The Ulster American Folk Park, Omagh 1967)

Garner, William *Historic Buildings in the Town of Cavan* (U.A.H.S. & An Taisce, Belfast & Dublin 1978)

Glin, The Knight of, David G. Griffin, & Nicholas K. Robinson, *Vanishing Country Houses of Ireland* (The Irish Architectural Archive & The Irish Georgian Society, Dublin 1988)

Gmelch, Sharon (ed.), *Irish Life* (The O'Brien Press, Dublin 1979)

Guinness, Mariga, 'The Deliberate Follies of Ireland' in *Ireland of the Welcomes*, Vol. XX, Jan./Feb. 1972

Hall, Mr & Mrs S.C., *Ireland, Its Scenery, Character, etc*, 3 vols (How and Parsons, London 1851–3)

Harbison, Peter, *Guide National Monuments Ireland* (Gill and Macmillan, Dublin 1970, reprinted)

Harbison, Peter, Homan Potterton & Jeanne Sheehy, *Irish Art and Architecture* (Thames and Hudson, London 1978)

Haughton, J.P., & others (eds.), *The Atlas of Ireland* (The Royal Irish Academy, Dublin 1979)

Horner, Arnold, 'Carton, Co. Kildare: A Case Study of the Making of an Irish Demesne' in *Irish Georgian Society Bulletin*, Vol. XVIII, 1975

Jones, Barbara, *Follies and Grottoes* (Constable Ltd, London 1953, revised and enlarged 2nd edn 1974)

Jackson, John A. & Liam Blake (photographer), *Irish Cottages* (Real Ireland Design Ltd., Wicklow 1985)

Kane, Sir Robert, *The Industrial Resources of Ireland* (Dublin 1845)

Lucas, A.T., 'Decorative Cobbling: examples from Counties Limerick, Wexford and Cork' in *Journal of*

Royal Society of Antiquaries of Ireland, Vol. 106, 1976, pp.31–72

McCutcheon, Alan, *Ireland* vol. 1, 1969; vol. 2, 1970, (David & Charles, Newton Abbot)

McCullough, Niall & Valerie Mulvin, A *Cost Tradition – The Nature of Architecture in Ireland* (Gandon Editions, Dublin 1978)

McParland, E., 'Sir Richard Morrison's Country Houses' in *Country Life*, May 1973

Malins, Edward & The Knight of Glin, *Lost Demesnes – Irish Landscape Gardening 1660–1845* (Barrie & Jenkins Ltd., London 1976)

Malins, Edward & The Knight of Glin, *Irish Gardens and Demesnes from 1830* (Barrie & Jenkins, London 1980)

Morrison, Sir Richard, *Useful and Ornamental Designs in Architecture (Villas)...* (1793)

Morrissey, James, *Inishboffin, Connemara* (Crannog Books, Dublin 1987)

National Heritage Inventory (An Foras Forbortha, Dublin, from 1979) – a listing of buildings in towns

O'Farrell, Fearghal, *Farm Buildings and the Environment* (An Foras Taluntais, Dublin 1987)

Orme, A.R., *The World's Landscapes 4: Ireland* (Longman Group Ltd., London 1970)

O'Riordain, Sean P., *Antiquities of The Irish Countryside* (Methuen and Co. Ltd., London 1942; University Paperback Edition 1965, reprinted 1971)

Prizeman, John, *Your House, The Outside View* (Hutchinson and Co., London 1975)

Praeger, R.L., *The Way That I Went* (Allen Figgis, Dublin 1980)

Price, Uvedale, *An Essay on the Picturesque* (1796)

Reid, Richard, *The Shell Book of Cottages* (Michael Joseph Ltd., London 1977)

Robinson, Philip, 'Vernacular Housing in Ulster in the Seventeenth Century' in *Ulster Folk Life*, vol. 25, 1979

Roche, Richard & Merne, Oscar, *Saltees – Islands of Birds and Legends* (The O'Brien Press, Dublin 1977)

Rothery, Sean, *Everyday Buildings of Ireland* (Department of Architecture, Bolton Street, Dublin 1975)

Rowan, Alistair, *The Buildings of Ireland: North-West Ulster*, Pevsner, Nikolaus, advisory ed. (Penguin Books, Harmondsworth 1979)

Shaffrey, Patrick & Maura, *Buildings of Irish Towns – Treasures of Everyday Architecture* (The O'Brien Press, Dublin 1983)

Shaffrey, Patrick & Maura, *Buildings of the Irish Countryside* (The O'Brien Press, Dublin 1985)

Shaffrey, Patrick, *The Irish Town – An Approach to Survival* (The O'Brien Press, Dublin 1975)

Shaw-Smith, David (ed.), *Ireland's Traditional Crafts* (Thames & Hudson, London 1984)

Sharkey, Olive, *Old Days Old Ways* (The O'Brien Press, Dublin 1985)

Sheehy, Jeanne, 'Railway Architecture', in *Irish Railway Record Society Journal*, Oct. 1975, p.125 sqq.

Stagles, Joan & Ray, *The Blasket Islands – Next Parish America* (The O'Brien Press, Dublin 1980)

Ulster Architectural Heritage Society, *Historic Buildings, Groups of Buildings, Areas of Architectural Importance* (U.A.H.S., Belfast from c. 1968) – architectural surveys of Ulster Towns and Counties

Weir, Hugh L., *Houses of Clare* (Ballinakella Press, Whitegate 1986)

Wilkinson, George, *Practical Geology and Ancient Architecture of Ireland* (John Murray, London 1845)

Wright, Lance, Kenneth Brown & Peter Jones, 'The Other Dublin' in *The Architectural Review* No. 933, Nov 1974, p.352 sqq.

Index